MW00581000

CULT T-SHIRTS

Published in 2022 by Welbeck
An imprint of Welbeck Non-Fiction Limited,
part of Welbeck Publishing Group
Based in London and Sydney.
www.welbeckpublishing.com

Text and design copyright © Welbeck
Non-Fiction Limited 2006, 2022

First published by Carlton Books in 2006

A CIP catalogue record for this book is available from the
British Library

Printed in Dubai

ISBN 978 1 80279 098 6

10 9 8 7 6 5 4 3 2 1

CULT T-SHIRTS

Over 500 rebel tees from the 70s & 80s

Phoebe Miller & Michael Reach

WELBECK

CONTENTS

FOREWORD

'One Friday morning back in 2000, too early to mention, after setting up my 1980s 'girl' stall at Portobello Road in London, I met Michael over a pink 1980s Playgirl T-shirt he was selling on his American vintage clothing stall. He'd picked the shirt up on a recent buying trip to Texas, he gave me £5 discount and we've never looked back.'

A book compiling classic vintage T-shirt designs from the years we love – that was the idea and the catalyst behind the book you're now holding. It sounded simple but we didn't realize the monster-sized volume of work it would become. Our aim was fairly straightforward; the T-shirts should speak for themselves – no lengthy descriptions or history lessons, just the facts. It's all about the shirts. The cut-off date is 1989. For us, this book is about T-shirt designs associated with youth movements, crazes and trends that relate to our youths and childhoods, in particular the 1970s and 1980s. Anything past 1989 doesn't have the same spark for us. We realize there were printed T-shirts way before the 1970s, but felt these should be covered in a separate volume.

The printed T-shirt has to be the most affordable form of art and the most direct method of self-expression of modern times.

T-shirts are walking billboards, easily accessible vehicles to exhibit one's identity, and with regard to social commentary, the shirts demonstrate a leaning towards specific youth movements or subcultures. They are classless and without boundaries. We want this book to be as accessible as the T-shirts were at the time they were first produced.

One of the hardest calls to make, once we'd gathered the vast selection, was in what specific order, if any, to feature the shirts. Chronologically? This made sense at first, but do you want to see a 1980s Day-Glo Vision Street Wear T-shirt alongside Madonna during her True Blue period? Not everyone will be satisfied with the categories – the whole project was laced with debates on who goes where. Most relevant to the music section, some purists may argue that certain acts are more rock than metal, more punk than new wave and so on. But ultimately this is a book of T-shirt design and not a lesson in rock history. The shirts are loosely grouped with the aim to capture a feeling in time and to suggest the mood of a youth scene.

We dug deep – from Paris to New York, from Denmark to back home in London – to cream off the supreme shirts you see in this book. Our quest led us to design archives, dealers, true fans and hardcore collectors alike. From our research, three types of T-shirt collector habits have emerged, and they seem to hold true across most genres of collecting, be it records, denim, trainers or books.

The museum collector: some addicts keep their tees tucked away in a darkened room, only to emerge for special occasions.

One for the road: these guys have got all angles covered – one tee to wear with confidence and another safely wrapped up and kept mint for the collection.

Till death: these T-shirt lovers buy shirts for what they are designed for – to be worn. Often they'll wear shirts till death, then they're crudely stitched back together and resurrected for a second wave.

Whatever the chosen method, we'd like to thank these fellow collectors, fans and brands for sharing their T-shirts with us. Without their help this task would not have been possible.

Take a close look at each T-shirt design for what it is – a piece of artwork – regardless of band or brand association. You'll find everything from graphically purist post-punk shapes to fantastical metal art; from crude cut-and-paste art school designs, to skull zombie line drawings, full 1980s neon colour to photographic hero-worship iron-ons. Enjoy the crazy mix!

INTRODUCTION

We're not claiming that this book is the definitive collection of printed tees, more like the tip of the iceberg of such a vast subject. There's still a mountain of used tees out there we wanted to show but we had to draw the line somewhere. Nor does this profess to be a collector's bible. It's an exploration of T-shirt art without prejudice.

The book includes some pretty obscure, rarely seen tees, alongside more commercial designs that were mass-produced. The important thing is that the artwork of both conjures up a feeling specific to a certain time in history and therefore they are considered, in this book, of equal importance graphically.

We've closed our ears to the music, put personal taste aside and opened our eyes to create an objective overview of 1970s and 1980s popular culture. All of the T-shirts included are original, pre-1989, pre-nostalgia trip trash that has saturated the market since the early 1990s, with comedy references to the past.

This book is a respectful genuine appreciation of the less self-conscious pioneering decades of the twentieth century.

Whether mint or moth-eaten, rare as hell or common as muck, screen-print or iron-on, consider this a celebration of some of the greatest printed T-shirt art of the 1970s and 1980s.

T-SHIRTS
THE STORY SO FAR

THE ROOTS

The T-shirt began life as a functional item of underwear designed not to be seen. In the early days it would have been considered offensive to reveal the shirt.

WW1

The origins of the T-shirt stem from Europe. During WW1, American soldiers were sweating in their woollen uniforms while their European counterparts were less restricted in their lightweight cotton undershirts.

WW2

The cotton T-shirt was standard issue as an undergarment in the US armed forces. WW2 also provided another preview of the T-shirt as soldiers crudely customized their vest-style tees to identify their station and using any materials they could find – often handmade, cut-out stencils and vehicle spray paint.

1940s AND 1950s

American colleges started printing their names and logos on tees; in the early days, normally using flock iron-on fonts. These were sold in the college stores on campus for students to wear with American pride. Later versions of these American university tees, such as Yale and Harvard, became a part of the early 1960s English mod look alongside other US Ivy League-style preppy garments.

The trend for small US businesses, such as garages, diners and electrical stores, to print their own logo or products on shirts for customers became common in the 1950s. They advertised brand loyalty in this way long before the major big league companies caught on. By the mid-1960s these 'walking billboard' advertising tees were big business.

Marlon Brando and James Dean shocked Americans by wearing their underwear on the big screen in *The Wild One* and *Rebel Without a Cause*. This marked the T-shirt's long-awaited progression from underwear to outerwear, infusing the style with a fashionable sex appeal at the same time. The rebel association was the catalyst for the style becoming a desirable item of clothing with the youth of the day and coincided with the birth of rock and roll.

1960s

The popularity of the printed rock-and-roll band shirt exploded in the 1970s, but the roots lie firmly in the 1960s. Although mid 1960s invasion-style groups dipped their toes in the T-shirt market, it was West Coast gig promoters, such as Bill Graham pushing local acts like the Grateful Dead, who first realized this emerging potential to sell T-shirts as well as gig tickets at venues.

1970s

The first wave of Sex Pistols and Clash fans, particularly those outside central London, had to take it upon themselves to create their own customized King's Road-esque creations. These do-it-yourself T-shirts were crudely vandalized and defaced using marker pens, tape, pins and zips.

SCREEN-PRINTS vs IRON-ONS

THE BATTLE OF THE T-SHIRT PRINT

SCREEN-PRINTS

The battle of the T-shirt print has been running for years. In collectors' circles the screen-printed tee is generally considered the most desirable, authentic and superior version of a vintage printed shirt. Arguably the main reason is that screen-prints were the only choice of official merchandisers at concerts and stadiums. They were mass-produced cheaply and easily, ready to be transported to venues worldwide. These tour shirts often featured an additional back print – never seen on an iron-on shirt – depicting the date, year and city of each individual concert. The ultimate 'I Was There' souvenir, its authenticity can't be matched. Another reason is the screen-prints' durability and the way in which it develops more character as it survives endless washes and wear and tear. The ink on a screened shirt is printed deep into the grain of the fabric, and the print ages gracefully over time, whereas rival iron-ons were printed on the surface of the shirt and developed a reputation for cracking and fading with wear.

Opposite: I Solved the Cube, an early 1980s US screen-print.

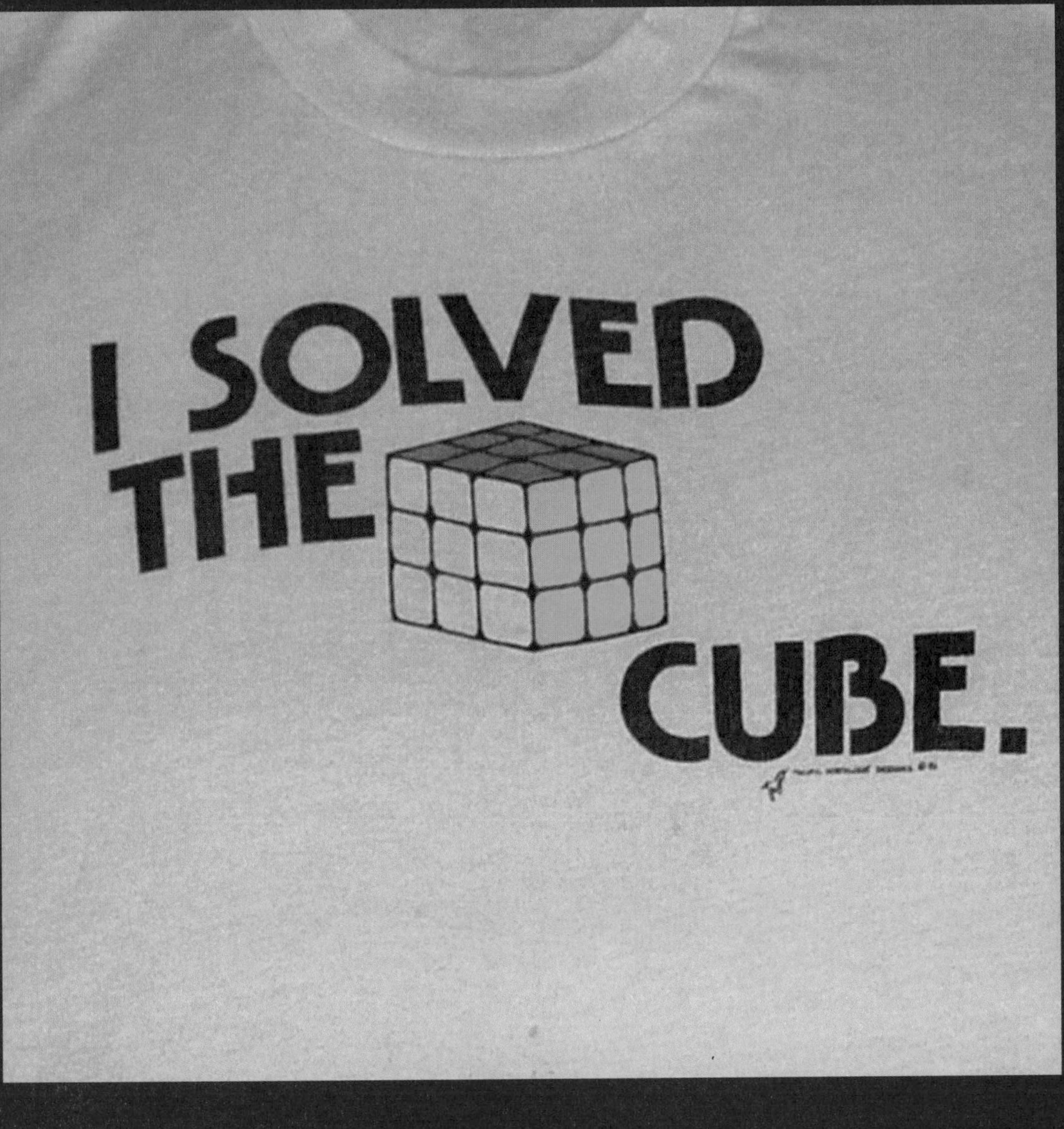
I SOLVED
THE
CUBE.

IRON-ONS

Back in the 1970s, you could walk into countless small T-shirt or gift shops across the UK and US and choose any of your favourite hit movies, rock stars, heart-throbs or cartoon characters and get them printed onto a blank shirt of your choice while you waited. In just minutes, you could be walking away with a one-of-a-kind tee. Popular themes of the day were covered – from fast cars, beer and drugs, to sexy pin-ups, lurid humour and astrological star signs.

One appeal of the transfer was the full colour, photographic image prints available, often with glitter borders. From Mr T to the Fonze, from Bowie to Black Sabbath, it was possible to have an actual photograph of your hero printed on your chest rather than the three-to-four colour artist's impression that was available on screen-printed shirts. Sadly, 1970s and 1980s transfers have often been seen as the poorer cousin of the screen-printed shirt. We feel they deserve a prominent place in T-shirt history and have included some fine examples of this lesser-appreciated art form.

Above: I Beat the Cube, an early 1980s transfer-printed shirt.

Opposite: Linda Lusardi, 1970s British 'Page 3' Girl and pin-up, promotes the while-you-wait appeal of the transfer-printed T-shirt. Featured in Imagine Transfers catalogue, circa 1982.

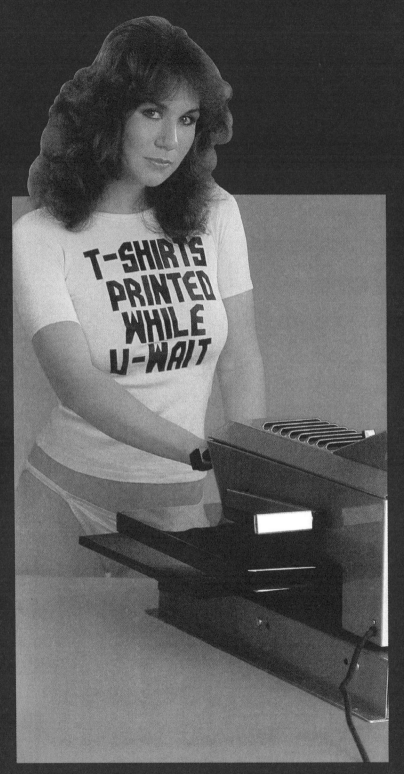

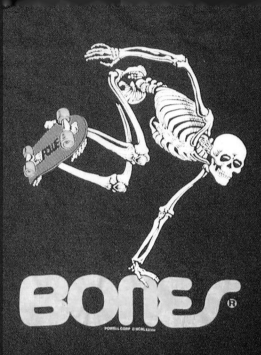

BONES

POWELL CORP. © MCMLXXVIII

SOUL KITCHEN

CHAPTER 1

THRASH 'N BURN

SKATE

Skate shirts became popular in the 1970s, but the graphics of the 1980s are considered to be the finest ever – electric colours, hardcore skulls and a real skate-punk crossover. This chapter includes a killer selection from the king brands of these classic years of radical T-shirt design.

'I feel like I saw the birth of skate rock in 1983. One Saturday night at the Tool & Die in San Francisco's mission district, *Thrasher* magazine got together the Scoundrelz (with Tony Alva), the Faction, Los Olvidados (my band) and JFA. My memories of the night are a swirl of Jak's SF skate teams and the SSG (Scurd Skate Gang) and possibly the CBS (City Boys Shred), all fucking with each other. It was like a scene out of a 1960s surf film, except there was no beach party. It was all about hardcore skaters getting super fucked up and swivelling (a dance that was part twisting and part skanking, less emphasis on slamming.) Mix in a bunch of suburban kids, add music, and everyone was raging.'

Ray Stevens, member of Los Olvidados

Opposite Mark 'Gator' Rogowski,
1980s vertical ramp skate legend.
Courtesy *STOKED: The Rise and Fall
of Gator*, © Joel Cherry.

Above and opposite: Skater Tom Groholski's
(known as the Jersey Devil) personal T-shirt,
front and back, from Vision Street Wear, 1988.

THRASHER

Skate was hungover from the 1970s and most magazines were merely treating it like a kid thing. *Thrasher* was different; it addressed what many skaters were really into – the punk rock/ skate punk element. It was raw. *Thrasher* featured bands of the day, but also the whole skate scene and what was really happening. More than just a fashion, it was a lifestyle. Their own tees were on the hardcore edge and summed up the period, particularly with artist/skater Pushead's skeleton designs. Their iconic logo has become a design classic in its own right.

Opposite and following pages: *Thrasher* magazine patch, mid to late 1980s and cover of the debut edition, January 1981.

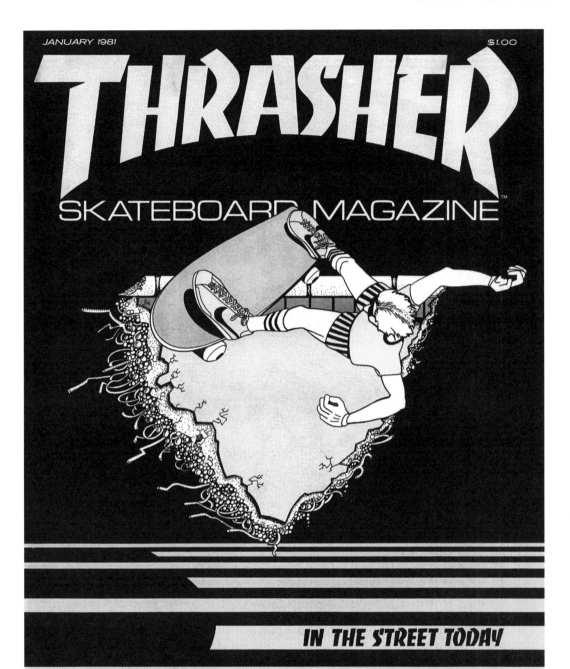

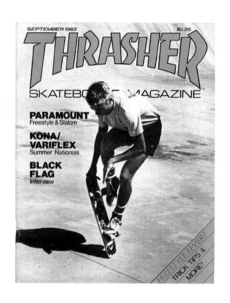

Above: An early 1980s T-shirt order form
featuring Randy 'Biskut' Turner from
Texas punk legends, the Big Boys.

Opposite: *Thrasher* magazine covers,
early to mid 1980s.

Opposite: Mid 1980s Thrasher T-shirt advertisement, including various Pushead designs.

Above: 'Thrashion' fashion, late 1980s Thrasher mail-order advertisement.

Above: A mid 1980s Thrasher logo shirt that once belonged to the legendary skater, Gator. Courtesy Helen Stickler.

Above: An early example of a classic
Thrasher logo tee, mid 1980s.

Above: Thrasher skate shirt by Pushead, mid 1980s. Artwork by Pushead summed up the hardcore skate-punk movement of the 1980s. His raw and horrific skull creature drawings covered just about everything connected with the scene, including boards, T-shirts, show flyers and record covers. Courtesy Helen Stickler.

Opposite: Early 1980s Thrasher mail-order advertisement.

BONES

Above left and right: Legendary skate crew Bones Brigade and Powell Peralta tie-in shirt, 1989. The '80s Powell Peralta label teamed George Powell, the godfather of skateboard manufacturing, and Stacy Peralta, film producer and original Z-boy.

Above left and right: Bones skeleton skater shirt, Powell Peralta, late 1980s.

Above and right: Bones logo design shirt and patch, Powell Peralta, late 1980s.

Above left and right: Jim Phillips-designed sponsorship
shirt for pro-skater Jeff Crosso, Santa Cruz, 1987.

Above left and right: Steve Caballero shirt by his board
sponsor at the time, Powell Peralta, 1986.

Above left and right: Pro-skater Corey O'Brien's flame-throwing reaper sponsorship shirt by Jim Phillips, Santa Cruz label, late 1980s

GATOR

Mark 'Gator' Rogowski was one of the most celebrated professional skateboarders of the 1980s. Performing during a period when local skatepark heroes were transformed into international superstars, he was sponsored by Vision Street Wear, who created some truly radical designs.

Above left and right: Off the Wall, Pipeline (Badlands) shirt, early 1980s.

Above: Gator's Pipeline membership card, 1984. The original Pipeline (also known as Badlands) in Upland, California was the first vertical skatepark in the world. It was also one of the most important Southern California skate scenes from the late 1970s through to the mid 1980s. Courtesy *STOKED: The Rise and Fall of Gator*.

Above: Off the Wall, Pipeline shirt, 1984. Courtesy Helen Stickler.

Opposite: Gator Rogowski, 1980s. Courtesy *STOKED: The Rise and Fall of Gator* and Bill Silva Productions.

Above: Vision Street Wear label, 1980s

Left: Spiral graphic Gator Vision Street Wear sponsorship advertisement, 1980s. Courtesy *STOKED: The Rise and Fall of Gator* and Vision Skateboards.

Above and Below: Gator/Vision promotional shirt (formerly belonging to Gator), late 1980s. Courtesy Helen Stickler.

Above: Gator/Vision long-sleeve shirt,
late 1980s. Courtesy Helen Stickler.

Above: Gator/Vision sponsorship shirt,
late 1980s. Courtesy Helen Stickler.

Above: Gator/Vision sponsorship advertisement, 1988.
The lurid, shock colours typify the mid to late 1980s
skate graphics. Courtesy *STOKED: The Rise and Fall
of Gator* and Vision Skateboards.

Opposite: The famous 1980s Jason Jessee Sun God
graphic – design by Jim Phillips – from his skateboard
sponsor at the time, Santa Cruz. Courtesy Helen Stickler.

Above and Opposite: Vision Street Wear
T-shirt, late 1980s. Courtesy Helen Stickler.

IRON-ONS

While the established skate companies were making T-shirts of
their own, transfer companies were also cashing in with their take
on the trend. Printed on generic, non-branded shirts, they were
not aimed at skaters, but rather for kids. Despite this, they still
sum up the style of mid to late 1980s skate graphics.

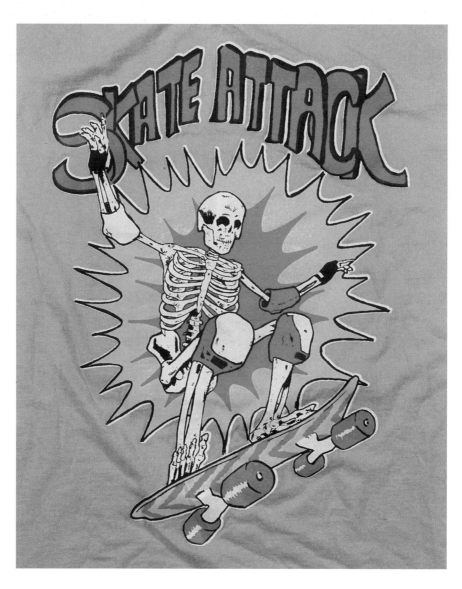

Opposite: Skate Attack, skating skeleton
iron-on shirt, 1985.

Above: Skate or Die iron-on shirt, mid to late 1980s.

Below: Thrash'n iron-on, aping the Thrasher logo,
from MBS Love transfers, US, 1985.

Above: Imitation Pushead punk
skeleton, 1988.

Above: Shred It!,
iron-on shirt, 1989.

COLLECTOR

FRANÇOIS DIRTY SOUTH ATLANTA, GEORGIA, US

PM: When and where did you first get into skate?

FDS: I must've been around 11 when I first got into skate. Before that I was into freestyle BMX, tricks and stuff. It was around 1985 or 1986, when pro-skater Rodney Mullen was doing a demo at Skate Eskape, down the street from my house. He was a freestyle skater with a real skinny board. He was doing kick flips, standing on his hands then flippin' to his feet. When I saw him skating, man, everything instantly changed. Biking faded out pretty fast and skate came into effect. It's funny, because I don't recall what music I was into when I was riding, but as soon as I was into skate, I knew what I was into – punk, hardcore, California skate punk, speed/thrash metal and all that stuff. I really explored the music because it all went together.

  This one day a local skate-punk band, Dead Elvis, were playing. They lived down the street from us so we all piled into the back of their truck with our boards. When we got there, there were kids skating out front, everywhere. We'd skate the curbs, then watch some bands, wearing our punk-rock gear. It was a lifestyle.

PM: Have you skated ever since?

FDS: It was around 1988 that skate started turning too commercial. We would still skate, but we weren't skaters. Boards got smaller, and by 1991 we would all joke to each other, 'What are these small boards with little wheels and these guys in baggy shorts?' Then it all stopped for me; it changed.

  Then in 1996 I moved to London and started skating again, but for transportation. I was wearing old skool Vans and flares, 1970s skate style; it started up again from there. But when I skate now I wear completely 1980s stuff – Dickies shorts, old skool Vans, maybe a Misfits shirt, an old hip bag and stuff.

  A mix of punk rock, skate punk and classic style. Now skates getting better for me as kids are getting into punk rock/skate rock and pros are getting back into old skool skating. A lot of old tricks are coming back, hand plants and that kind of stuff, on the ground, dirty and hardcore.

PM: You've got a wild skate tee collection, can you pick a favourite shirt?

FDS: Yeah, my favourite is a hot pink Per Welinder, a Swedish freestyle skater, circa 1984 by Powell Peralta. It's a sample, a guy got it for me deadstock in California.

PM: Do you keep it stored in mint condition?

FDS: With shoes, they get burnt out, but shirts keep gettin' better. When I wear the Per Welinder skating, especially in the States, people just freak out, stop and say, 'Where d'you get that shirt?'

  Another of my most prized shirts is the Gator Vision shirt. It's way too big to wear, but I can put it up on my wall. It's from the day and, wow, it's one of the things I could never sell.

PM: Is there a period in skating from which you collect specifically? Do you think that skate peaked in a certain year?

FDS: New stuff just has no style – small prints on big and baggy shirts. The best shirt graphics for me were from 1981 to 1988 – real skate, punk, hardcore, skulls, zombies and stuff. In 1988 to 1989 the graphics started to turn – less skulls and more hip hop; the whole scene was changing. It all softened up and in some ways it went cartoon and less evil. It still had it's own style, but you lived to be skater punk.

PM: You deal in skate stuff, too. How do you work out what to keep and what to part with?

FDS: I've had shitloads of stuff from 1988 to 1992, when the artwork was softer. That's easier as it's not my thing. It's harder with the 1981 to 1988 stuff, I'm into that. My biggest regret is selling a pink Tony Hawk shirt, dated 1984. I sold it to a collector, an English guy with a sick amount of skate stuff. He was a bigtime collector. I sold it for £75 – man, that was too cheap, looking back. If you want to do business, you can't keep everything, but I should have kept hold of that shirt.

Above: MA1 jacket signed by Bones Brigade members Ray Barbee and Steve Saiz on their 1989 world tour.

Opposite: Powell Peralta shirt, mid 1980s.

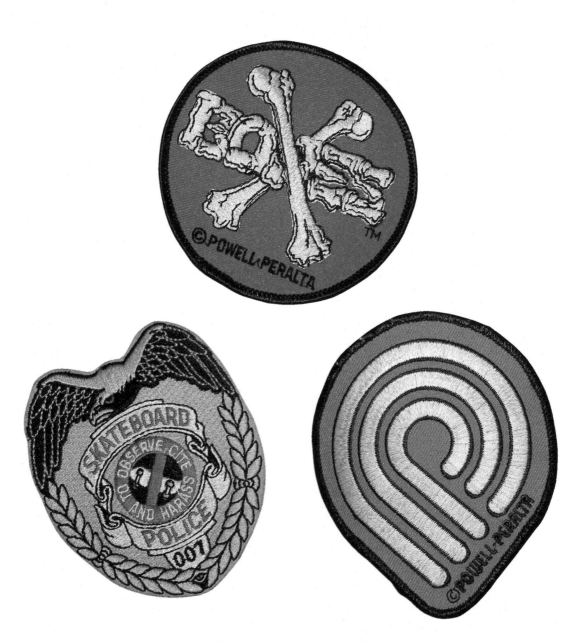

Above and Opposite: Skate patches and front view of the MA1 jacket, 1980s.

Above and Opposite: Sims Pure
Juice shirt, late 1970s.

Above left and right: Lance Mountain shirt, Powell Peralta, 1985.

Below left and right: Tony Alva's own Variflex shirt. 'In 1978, West Coast US came to West Country UK. Legendary Dogtown skater, Tony Alva, found himself the centre of attention, skating a ridiculous 30-foot tall, four-foot wide mobile half-pipe built on the back of a low-loader at the Royal Bath and West Show (normally reserved for pigs, sheep and dog trials) in the heart of agricultural England. I was lucky enough to grab this shirt when he threw it into an avalanche of adoring 12-year-old kids.' – Matthew Hawker

Above and below: Hobie skateboard promotional
shirt, 1987. Courtesy Helen Stickler.

Above, below and opposite: One of the most famous images from 1980s skateboarding is, without question, the Screaming Hand design. Created by artist Jim Phillips for the Santa Cruz label, the design was first sketched in 1985. The shirt dates from the late 1980s.

STÜSSY

In the late 1980s a phenomenon swept through the clothing scene that produced a label that redefined the previous notions of casualwear. That label was Stüssy. Shawn Stüssy was a surfer who used to shape his own boards for friends and locals in Laguna Beach, California. The logo he used was his surname written in graffiti tag style and it wasn't very long before he was screening his own T-shirts and shorts to sell along with the surfboards as a form of promotion. This was just the beginning… Design images featured '50s Americana, black-and-white photos of skate kids rocking the b-boy styles of the time, and they all bore the trademark Stüssy handwritten style. It's not easy to convey just how fresh and innovative they looked at the time, as there was nothing like it available. It had that elusive X-factor that makes the difference between a good piece and an amazing one.

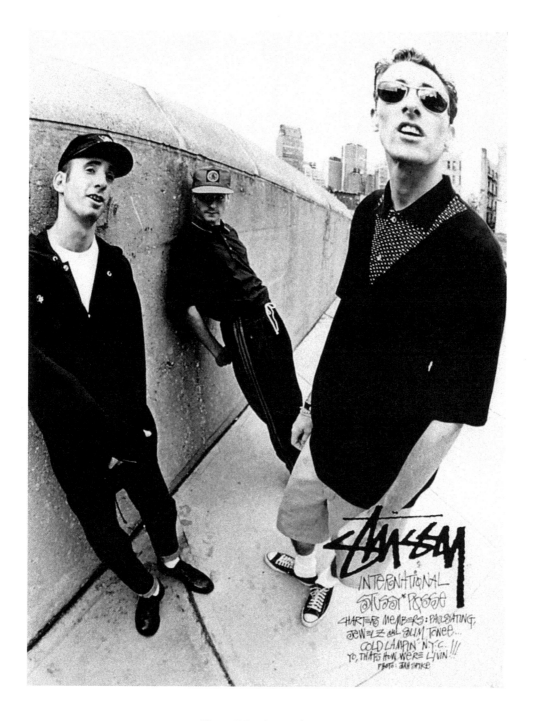

Above: Stüssy New York posse
advertisement, 1989.

Above: One of Stüssy's endlessly evolving logo print designs, late 1980s

Below: Chairman Mao, Charlie Don't Surf design, late 1980s.

CHARLIE DON'T SURF...

Above: Okay Big Boys, Shut Up and Do
Your Thang!! Stüssy shirt, 1989.

Below: Chairman Mao, Charlie Don't
Surf design, late 1980s.

Above: Kid Dred shirt, No Follow No Fashion Monkey…
Dis Ain't No Puppy Dog Show, 1989.

Below: Stüssy scooter couple, late 1980s.

Opposite: Stüssy's New York City Crew
advertisement, late 1980s.

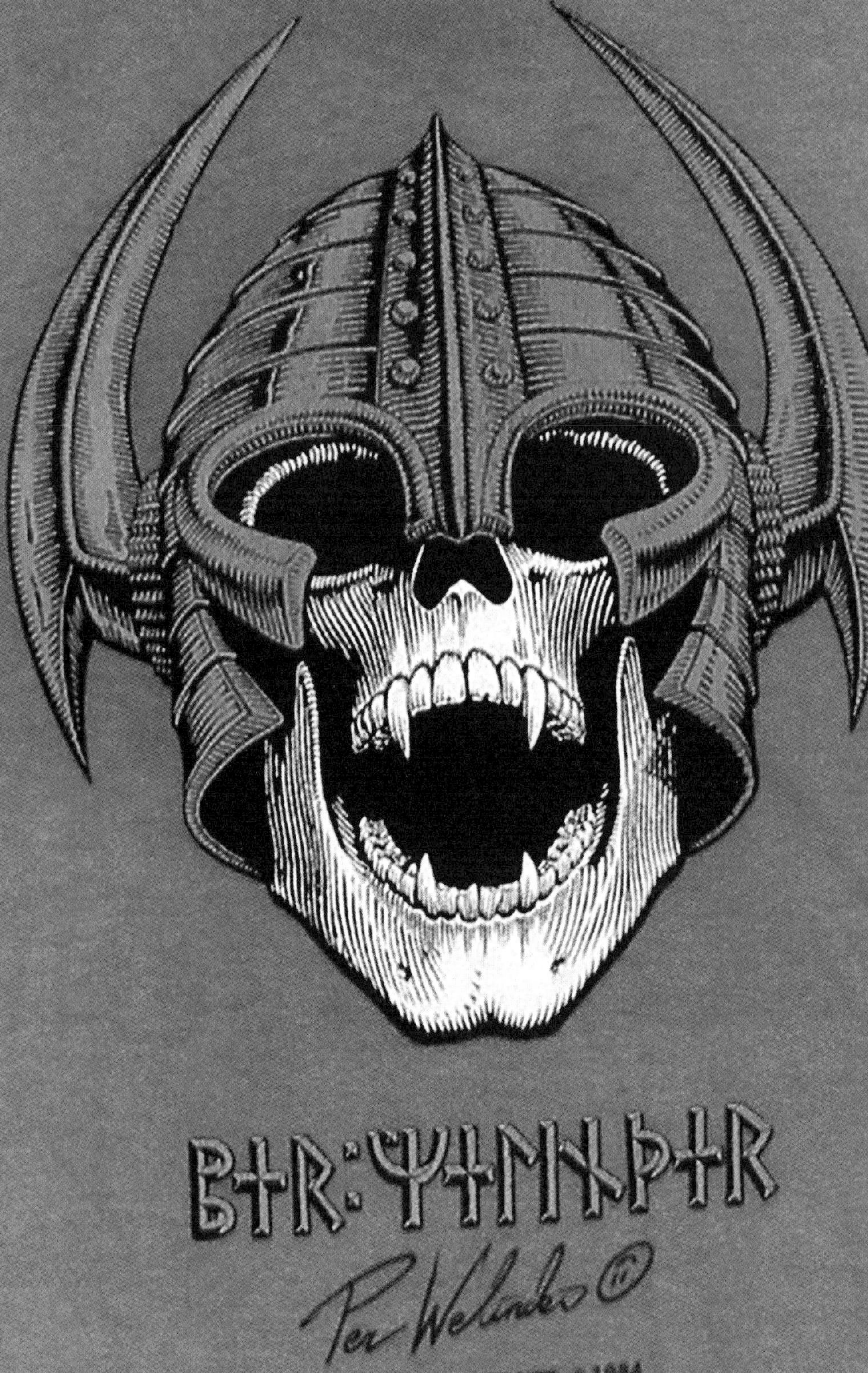
Per Welinder
POWELL PERALTA © 1984

Opposite: Swedish freestyle skater, Per Welinder's sample shirt by Powell Peralta, 1984.

Above left and right: Brand X skate company shirt, 1987.

Below left and right: Mike McGill's Powell Peralta sponsorship shirt, 1987.

Opposite above and centre: Hang Ten ringer shirt and label, mid 1970s.

Opposite below: Ramp skater shirt, Vision Street Wear, 1987.

Above and right: Vision Aggressor shirt, 1986.

COLLECTOR

CAMMO PETE
LONDON, UK

PM: What was skating to you, as a kid in the 1970s?

P: I got into skating when I was really young, you know, probably around seven or eight. I made a skateboard out of some wood and the wheels from some roller skates. It was the boom of the 1970s when I got my first shop-bought board and that's when I got really into it. It was hard to get the gear in England at the time though; only a few kids had it and they either knew people in the States or had rich parents.

I used to buy these mags that had all this crazy stuff in them. I'd go into a frenzy about it. It was so far removed from anything we had or could have – wild stuff. My Holy Grail was a Hobie Park Rider. I'd look at the pictures and my eyes would be like saucers, taking it all in.

I wore Dunlop Black flash plimsoles with Levi's and a T-shirt from the local market. Later, I got into punk and would wear band shirts – the Damned, Pistols and stuff. I'd also make my own shirts with zips and leopard print on them. Nothing was skate specific and it was all really expensive back then in comparison with today. In relative terms it was double the price, and we were kids with no income.

In 1976, we moved to Peterborough and I used to skate around the estate with local kids. We used to go to the playground and skate the concrete banks around the slides. At weekends there was a roller rink. We would go down and the place would be rammed with kids skating. That was our Dogtown – we didn't have swimming pools to skate.

We used to save up our pocket money and get a coach to London, then we'd go and skate at Southbank. Everybody would be looking sharp and we'd be the scraggly out-of-town kids. It was in 1976 when I saw my first pro-skater, John Sablosky. When I saw him, I thought it was the most fucking insane thing ever. We'd seen him in magazines – to see someone that hooked up, it just blew us away.

Skate to me was about freedom of expression. Freedom to create and use all that youthful aggression in a positive way. That's what we wanted as kids – something you could be good at, but that wasn't safe. And it didn't have that jock thing, you didn't have to be part of a team. You'd do it with others, but you'd be skating on your own.

Above and opposite: Palm Sunset
T-shirt, Ocean Pacific, 1986.

BEACH SHIRTS

Beach shirts evolved in the 1940s and 1950s in the US, largely for the teen market. This chapter picks up on the laidback, hazy and often romantic shirt designs of the 1970s and 1980s, the free and easy way of life that epitomized the endless summer spirit of the beach lifestyle.

Above: Hawaii beach T-shirt, late 1970s.

Below: Hawaii Hang Loose, 1980.

Above: Hawaii shirt, late 1970s.

Below: Sea-god beach shirt, mid 1970s.

Above left: Surf iron-on T-shirt, 1974.

Above right: Hawaii iron-on transfer T-shirt, Imagine transfers, 1984.

Below left: Hawaii glitter iron-on shirt, Roach transfers, 1974.

Below right: Hang On iron-on shirt, Roach transfers, 1974.

Above: Gold Coast glitter iron-on
transfer T-shirt, 1981.

Above: Surf sunset iron-on shirt, Roach transfers, 1974.

Below: Beach Bunny iron-on, early 1970s.

Above: Surfer scene iron-on, Wildside transfers, 1980.

Below: Surf scene, early 1980s.

Above: Surf block-letter shirt, mid 1980s.

Below and opposite: The original Panama Jack surf shirt, late 1980s.

OCEAN PACIFIC

Ocean Pacific (OP) originated in the 1960s as a surfboard label. In 1972, its founder, Jim Jenks, created an apparel line that met the demands of surfers both in and out of the water. From then on, the brand quickly became the definitive name in the surf/beach culture.

By the end of the 1970s, the youth market had come of age: it was no longer just a counterculture. Young people in America were now the dominant power behind music, film, sports and entertainment. They had the necessary disposable income to make a company like OP a major player in the fashion market. And over the next decade OP became just that – a household name and an icon of the West Coast lifestyle.

All Ocean Pacific shirts courtesy of Ocean Pacific design archives.

Above and right: Geometric Flowers, Ocean Pacific, mid 1980s.

Opposite: Abstract Surfer, Ocean Pacific, mid 1980s.

Left and below: Beach Style, Ocean Pacific, mid 1980s.

Opposite above: Abstract Wave, Ocean Pacific, mid 1980s.

Opposite below: Sunset Palm scene, Ocean Pacific, early 1980s.

Above and below: Surf Rider, Ocean Pacific, late 1970s.

Above: Sunset Palm polo shirt, Ocean Pacific, 1976.

Below: Rainbow Palm polo shirt, Ocean Pacific, late 1970s.

Above: Surf Horizon polo shirt, Ocean Pacific, mid 1970s.

Above: Surf Couple polo shirt, Ocean Pacific, 1975.

Above: Floral Rainbow polo shirt, Ocean Pacific, mid 1970s.

Above: Surfer polo shirt, Ocean Pacific, late 1970s.

Above left and right: Neon Rider,
Ocean Pacific, late 1980s.

Below left and right: Wave Surfer,
Ocean Pacific, early 1980s.

Opposite: Detail of Abstract Surfer,
Ocean Pacific, early 1980s.

BMX

BMX, or bicycle moto-cross to give it its full name, started out in the late 1960s. Californian kids, too young to ride moto-cross bikes, raced their bicycles on dirt tracks, trying desperately hard to be radical. Eventually a few parents became involved, and soon races were organized, and the bicycles engineered for greater strength and speed.

The sport of BMX racing began in the early 1970s. From that point on, a renaissance in the bicycle industry took place. As the sport grew, this 'new big thing from California' spread across the world. BMX bikes as we now know them appeared at the start of the 1980s, and from there the craze really went wild. Doing tricks – freestyle – became hugely popular and was probably most famously captured in the film *E.T.* (1982).

Because BMX was born as the younger brother of moto-cross, it was heavily influenced by skateboarding, surfing and the carefree, outdoors attitude prevalent across southern California at the time. BMX is continually evolving, but one aspect remains constant – the two wheels, the basic BMX layout and the simplicity of being on a bike; essentially it's all about skids and wheelies.

Opposite: Youth BMX iron-on advertisement
for Target transfers, 1984.

Above: BMX Kuwahara iron-on, Target transfers, 1983.

Above: BMX Mongoose, Target transfers, 1984.

Below: BMX Winner, Target transfers, 1984.

Above and below: Freestylin' riding T-shirt, 1989.

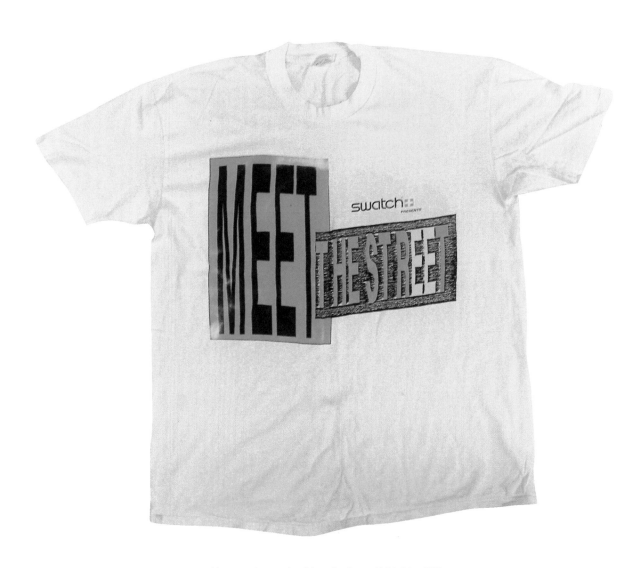

Above and opposite: Meet the Street BMX shirt, 1987.

Above and right: Freestyle BMX, 1989.

Opposite: Soul Kitchen, 2B, 1989. Underground American BMX and riding label 2B was set up by friends Hal Brindley and Steve Buddendeck, the two Bs.

COLLECTOR

**MARK NOBLE, EDITOR, RIDE BMX MAGAZINE,
DORCHESTER, ENGLAND**

PM: Were you already into bikes before you got into BMX?

MN: Yes. I've always been into bikes, from a very early age. Hareing around the village as a kid on various bikes, I was always into two wheels… then, as soon as BMX bikes started coming over here [to the UK] in 1980, my brother Chris and I got straight into it. That was it from then on; I never looked back.

PM: What about BMX most appealed to you?

MN: Simplicity, fun, durable, jumpable and chuckable. You could modify them, tart them up, ride from dawn till dusk without a care in the world.

PM: You have some great T-shirts. Are there any shirts you're after and would go all out for?

MN: I think, since I was so influenced by the magazine at the time, I'd love to get some of the original *BMX ACTION* magazine T-shirts from the early 1980s, in mint condition. That magazine had the best logo in the history of BMX; it was an American magazine, and the shirts were hard to get hold of here in Blighty.

PM: Do you only collect shirts or all BMX stuff?

MN: I'm into all BMX stuff – bikes, parts and hardware development – but shirts are the most accessible item, I guess… And they never crack.

PM: Can you remember your first BMX T-shirt?

MN: Yes. A Strongs Bicycles race shirt. Strongs was a great little BMX shop in Bournemouth, where my first BMX bike came from.

PM: How many BMX T-shirts do you own?

MN: Enough to fill about five suitcases. And I've only kept the best ones and thrown tons away that were no good.

PM: Do you wear them all, or do you store them away, collector style?

MN: I wear a lot of them, but the older ones are stored in the loft in cases – if they're too small, too extra large, or too holey…

PM: Do you have a favourite tee with a story behind it?

MN: I guess my *FREESTYLIN'* magazine T-shirt [see page 101], given to me by Andy Jenkins while on a visit to the offices in LA back around 1991. It has a great graphic wraparound logo and it's in one piece, so I still wear it today.

PM: You work in an office with a half pipe in it! So I guess you're still as excited about the scene now as when it first started?

MN: The BMX scene is so different to how it was back in the 1980s. Back then, racing was the big thing – now, it's riding street, trails, skateparks, flatland, racing and vert. There's so much choice and riders are so into it now. Back then it was a fledgling sport, but now it's an established lifestyle; riders live for it. I'm totally into it, every day is consumed by BMX by the sheer nature of my work – if I didn't like it, I wouldn't do it! Simple as that. I still ride when I can, go to as many BMX events as I want to, and I'm psyched when I see people riding. It's all about the riding.

PM: Do you feel the scene peaked in the 1980s? Or is it still moving forward?

MN: In terms of simple numbers, more people were riding BMX in the craze days of the 1980s, but the actual riding being done then, compared to today, was so basic. Now BMX is an established part of the scene – it's no longer misunderstood or thought of as a childish craze.

PM: Do you think BMX is at the start of a major revival?

MN: I doubt it. Kids are too spoilt these days and have a massive choice – computer games, MP3 players, television, DVD players, mobile phones, phone tones, Internet… It's a wonder they actually get outdoors and do something physically active. Riders my age never had that choice – we had BMX, or a space hopper, or a hula hoop. No wonder it boomed like crazy in the 1980s. Though riders who ride BMX are down for life. So from that standpoint, BMX is stronger now than before.

Above: On Any Sunday, classic Steve McQueen
dirt bike film shirt, early 1970s.

Above: Great Britannia BMX jersey shirt, 1986.

Above: US BMX shirt, old Hanes' label tee, 1979/1980.

Above: SE (Scot Enterprises) Racing, early 1980s.

Below: S&M Bikes, the King of Bikes, 1989.

Above: Bad Bicycles and Dirt road-sign shirt, 1989.

Opposite: UK BMX shirt, mid 1980s.

Opposite: Freestyle Masters, Vision Street Wear, 1986.

Above: Evolution, 1989.

Above and below: Homecooked logo shirt, 2B, 1989.

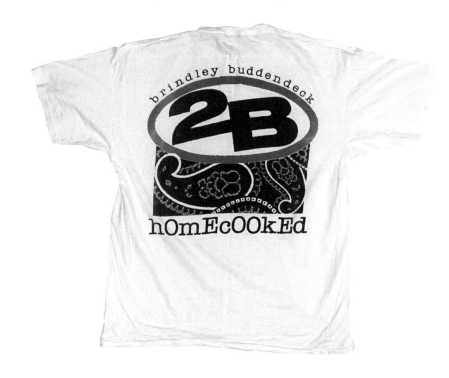

Above and below: Alternative Homecooked shirt, 2B, 1989.

2-HIP

The 2-Hip trick team started back in 1983 during the time when BMX freestyle was just beginning, with riders Ron Wilkerson and Rich Avella in northern California. In 1986, to fill a need for competitions representing the newer styles of riding, pro-rider Ron Wilkerson began organizing the first BMX Vert half-pipe series called the 2-Hip King of Vert and the first-ever BMX street jams, called the 2-Hip Meet the Street series. 2-Hip products started with T-shirts in 1986, including the ever-popular pink-and-green Dave Carson-designed logo shirts, and a member's only group called the 2-Hip Society. The business continues today with American-made parts and frame sets and a full line of complete bikes.

2-HIP RULES!

YEP, 2-HIP FOR '89

B the first with new 2-HIP stuff! Beat the rush! **SEE NEW SHIRTS ON PAGE 64!**

- Meet the Street logo shirt$12+$2
- Riders never Die shirt $12+$2
- original 2-HIP logo shirt $12+$2
- K.O.V. logo shirt $12+$2
- **JOIN** for '891 B in the HIP club! Get new shirt, stickers, cap, & quarterly 2-HIP zine for a year! $15+$3.50

- 89 CATALOGUE $1
- 2HIP sticker $1 brand new!
- 2HIP BIG STCKER $3.50
- 2-HIP LOGO sticker $1
- BIG 2-HIP sticker $3.50
- K.O.V. LOGO sticker $1
- BIG K.O.V. sticker $3.50
- K.O.V. poster $3.50 + 1.50
- 87 series video - a few left!

$19.99+3

88 series video & final video out next month!

SEND NAME, ADDRESS, SIZE and CHECK OR MONEY ORDER TO: 2-HIP P.O. 4065 LEUCADIA, CA 92024 619-753-7697 foreign orders add $4- READY to ship!

DON'T MISS THESE EVENTS!

	STREET	K.O.V.
MAY 27-28 WOODWARD, PA	✓	✓
JULY 22 COLORADO SPRINGS		✓
AUGUST TBA NEW YORK CITY	✓	✓
NOVEMBER 11 PORTLAND		✓
DECEMBER 5 SAN DIEGO		✓

photo - 2-HIP in TORONTO

Opposite: 2-Hip, King of Vert, Carson-designed shirt, 1987.

Above: 2-Hip Rules!, mail-order advertisement, 1989.

2hip

meetTHEstreet
aPril sixteenth
laJolla, CA

senD 100¢ for cat
alogue and iNnfo
  2 H I P
p.O.bOx 4065
  LEucadiA, CaL.
619.7537697
zIp:92024

jOinTHEs o c i ety
  4 eightyniNe.
sEnd $15. +$3.50 poSt.
  doitNOW.

carsondesign

120

Opposite: 2-Hip Meet the Street advertisement, 1989.

Above and below: Wilkerson Airlines shirt, 1989.
2-Hip began producing Wilkerson Airlines-branded BMX
products for hardcore riders in the late 1980s.

Above and opposite: 2-Hip advisory stamp shirt, late 1980s.

CHAPTER 2

FEEL THE NOIZE

LET IT ROCK

Rock is arguably the biggest thing to ever happen to the printed T-shirt. Born in the 1950s, rock fever spread like wildfire in the 1960s and by the '70s more records were being sold than ever before. The popular youth music of the day found mass appeal the world over. Rock merchandising became fashionable business, as it was all the rage to flaunt your taste in notes and chords on your chest. Rock is such a broad genre – from the progressive rock of Pink Floyd and the glam rock of Slade to the heavy rock of Led Zeppelin and the acid rock of the Grateful Dead – and we've tried to touch on all substyles beneath this vast umbrella. Rock forth and feast your eyes on a magic mix of classic rock tees.

Above left: Yardbirds, 1966. This shirt was originally owned by the late, great Greg Shaw and was worn at the Monterey festival in 1967.

Above right: The Who band logo shirt, 1974.

Above: The Who tie-dye shirt, 1970, worn
by Keith Moon on the cover of the album
Meaty Meaty Big and Bouncy, 1971.

Above: Mott the Hoople iron-on thermal-style T-shirt, 1972.

Below: Allman Brothers Band logo shirt, early 1970s.

Above: A Mercury Records promo shirt for Blue Ash,
an underrated Ohio power-pop band, 1972.

Below: Slade, Cum On Feel the Noize,
silver glitter iron-on, 1973.

Above: Bloodrock, American hard rock group of 'DOA' single fame, 1971.

Below: Led Zeppelin glitter iron-on band shirt, early 1970s.

Above: Free, London blues-rock group, early 1970s.

Below: Todd Rundgren, Go Ahead, Ignore Me!, glitter screen-print shirt, early 1970s.

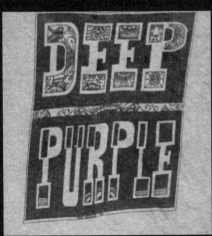

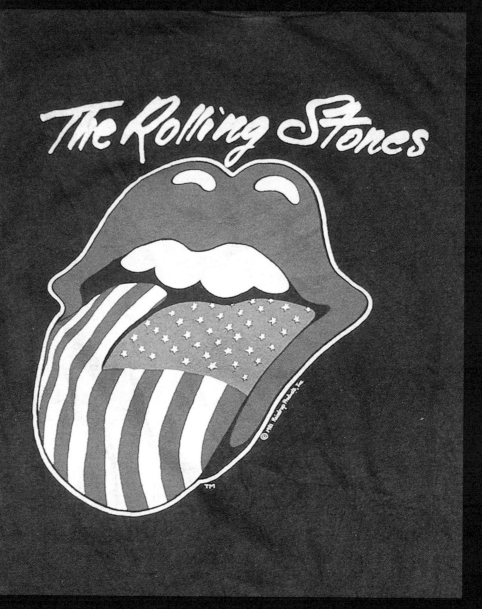

Opposite above: Bee Gees, Spirits Having Flown tour, 1979

Opposite below left: Deep Purple, 1973/1974

Opposite below right: Jackson Browne, 1974;

Above: Rolling Stones, US tour, 1981.

Above: Loggins and Messina, *Sitting In* album artwork T-shirt, 1971

Below: Bruce Springsteen, *Darkness on the Edge of Town* period, 1978

Opposite above: The Beatles, *Sgt Pepper's Lonely Hearts Club Band* music film promo shirt, 1978

Opposite below: Emerson Lake & Palmer, eponymous first-album artwork shirt, 1971.

Above: Dr Pepper Central Park Music Festival, 1978.

Opposite above: Beach Boys, 1973

Opposite below left: Elton John, 1973–1974

Opposite below right: Slade logo, 1972

Above: Led Zeppelin, 1973
Below: Bee Gees, 1975

Above: The Kinks, 1974

Below: Schaefer Music Festival, 1975

Above: Mick Jagger, All Right, iron-on pin-up shirt, 1976.

Below: Mick Jagger iron-on shirt, early 1970s.

Above: Mick Jagger, All Right, iron-on pin-up shirt, 1976.

Below: Pink Floyd, photographic-edged iron-on, 1975

Left and below: Pink Floyd, Animals tour shirt, 1977.

Opposite above: Grateful Dead, spring concert at Amherst, Massachusetts, with Patti Smith Group and Roy Ayres Ubiquity, May 1979.

Opposite below: Grateful Dead, Rock & Roll Will Never Die, Syracuse, New York tour, 1984.

Above and below: Grateful Dead, European tour jersey shirt, 1981. The Dead were one of the first groups to set the trend for printing band T-shirts in the late 1960s.

EDINBURGH, SCOTLAND 30 SEPTEMBER
LONDON, ENGLAND   2, 4 & 6 OCTOBER
COPENHAGEN, DENMARK 8 OCTOBER
BREMEN, GERMANY   10 OCTOBER
MÜNCHEN, GERMANY   12 OCTOBER
RÜSSELSHEIM, GERMANY 13 OCTOBER
NANCY, FRANCE   14 OCTOBER
FREJUS, FRANCE   16 OCTOBER
PARIS, FRANCE   17 OCTOBER
BARCELONA, SPAIN   19 OCTOBER

1981 EUROPEAN TOUR

Above and below: Grateful Dead,
Jungle Weekend ringer shirt, 1978.

Above and opposite: The Beach Boys in Concert,
25th Anniversary tour shirt, 1985.

Opposite above: The Eagles, Long Run tour shirt, late 1970s.

Opposite below: A montage of classic Grateful Dead skull-based illustrations, 1979/1980.

Above and right: Tom Petty and the Heartbreakers, Live in Concert, cut-off jersey shirt, 1979.

Above: Billy Joel, mid 1970s

Below: ZZ Top, the 'Little 'Ole Band from Texas', early 1970s

Above: Wings, Over America tour, 1976

Below: Carole King, early 1970s

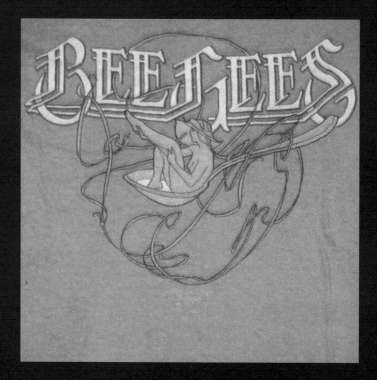

Above: Bee Gees, *Main Course* album-artwork promo shirt, 1975

Below: Beatles, Let It Be NY festival shirt, 1970s

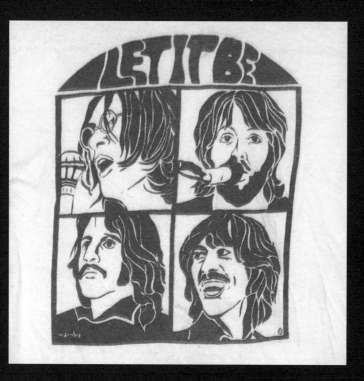

Above: Dr Pepper Music Festival on the Pier, 1981

Below: The Beatles, *Sgt Pepper's Lonely Hearts Club Band*, 1978

Above: AC/DC, Bon Scott memorial iron-on, 1980.

Opposite above: Black Sabbath, 1970s.

Opposite below: Ozzy Osbourne, early 1980s.

Opposite: Kiss, Rock 'n Roll Over tour shirt, 1976–1977. The tee was purchased at the band's historic first-time performing at Madison Square Garden, New York City, February 1977.

Above and right: Kiss, Love Gun tour shirt, 1978. The *Love Gun* album artwork appears on the front of the shirt, while the back design is based on a famous press photo of the band, circa 1977.

Above and opposite: A very early unofficial Kiss shirt from 1977. Owned by Jon Rubin (see pages 160–165), it was probably won at a state fair carnival, rather than purchased at a Kiss concert. Note that the back of the shirt is printed in reverse, since the star painted on Paul Stanley's eye is on the wrong side – a common problem with the bootleg T-shirts.

COLLECTOR

JON RUBIN
NEW YORK, US, WWW.KISSROCKS.NET

PM: Your Kiss collection is mindbending. When and how did you first get into Kiss music?

JR: Funny you should ask that, being that I can't remember a time when I *wasn't* into Kiss! It really stems back to my older brother literally taping pictures of all the members of the band onto my baby crib, probably sometime in 1975. A few years later, when Kiss was at their peak in the US, I could hear their music playing from my brother's room constantly and I loved the excitement and energy it possessed. I have distinct memories of sneaking into his room at the tender age of four and just staring at the colourful *Rock 'n Roll Over* and *Love Gun* album covers, which visually captured what the band was all about. My parents bought me the Kiss toy guitar in 1977 and it wasn't long before I was playing jumping around with it on tables and couches at any and

Above: A Kiss shirt from their Dynasty tour, 1979. Despite the shirt reading 'World Tour 1979' this shirt never made it off American soil due to the lukewarm response to the *Dynasty* album. The 1979 Dynasty tour marked drummer Peter Criss's last tour with the group and the end of the original line-up, not counting 1990's reunion. This shirt was available through the band's official fan club, the Kiss Army.

all family functions, singing and air-guitaring to my favourite Kiss tunes. Just a year or two later, I was dragging my folks to the local record store to buy the new Kiss album for me. Between their fun, exciting music and intense comic book/horror imagery, you could say I was intrigued. Looking back on it now, almost 30 years later, I still understand exactly what it was that got me hooked at such a young age.

PM: What makes collecting Kiss so special?

JR: Kiss is truly one of the few bands who make collecting fun. They had four individual members who each had their own fans (partially modelled after the Beatles), so you have to realize that with Kiss everything is multiplied four times because everything came as a set of four. Sure, that's four times the money to spend, but also four times the coolness factor – a genius plan for sure! And their T-shirts were particularly striking because, just like their album covers and posters, they always featured the band members on the front accompanied by the prominent Kiss logo, always in bright colours and mesmerizing presentation. Because they were so marketable, it's no surprise that they were (and still are) one of the most merchandised bands in the history of music. Years after the original line-up has come and gone (twice now), the likenesses of the original four Kiss characters continues to be licensed and merchandised worldwide, which is a testament to the power of the branding they created. There are many other bands whose music and style I love and appreciate, but I would never think to collect anything of theirs, simply because there's no excitement to it.

PM: Do you collect any tees from other bands? Or are you a one-band guy?

JR: Kiss and only Kiss – I bought other shirts from other rock concerts I went to in the 1980s, and wore many of them at the time, but I never actually collected T-shirts of other groups simply because none of them had Ace, Gene, Peter or Paul on them!

PM: Do you remember your first Kiss concert or T-shirt?

JR: Absolutely. They're one and the same, March 9, 1984 at Radio City Music Hall in New York City. It was Kiss's big homecoming gig for the Lick It Up tour after taking off their make-up and, fittingly enough, my older brother (who got me into the band in the first place) surprised me with tickets and took me to the show. It was there that I bought my first Kiss T-shirt – a 1983–84 double-sided black tour tee, which was the ultimate souvenir of such a memorable and important night. Although we had terrible seats, I had the time of my life because

Above: A shirt from the Kiss Asylum tour, 1985–1986.

I had been waiting to see them live for many years – and I have this concert T-shirt to prove I was there.

PM: What's on your 'wants' list? Is there a T-shirt out there you've never managed to get your hands on?

JR: There are many cool Kiss shirts from the 1970s that are hard to find and would probably be very expensive if located. I'm always keeping my eyes out for the super rare set of shirts offered from the 1978 solo album order forms (a simple single-sided black shirt with each member's face on the front – just $5 back then!). Also anything from the 1980 Unmasked tour, since the majority of that tour was overseas and featured the new drummer Eric Carr – two reasons that would make those shirts more collectible. I'd also really like any Kiss jersey with the three-quarter sleeves, a style/trend specific to only a few of their tours in the early to mid 1980s and therefore increasingly hard to find.

PM: Do you ever wear your shirts or do you store them away in a special place?

JR: I never wear any of the shirts, mostly because they would never fit these days! But truthfully, some of them feel so fragile that I hesitate to even handle them, let alone wear them. I don't see how the value could ever be preserved by wearing them. As for the caring of them, I don't store them in any special way; I just fold them neatly and keep them in a pile with the rest of my Kiss collection. And yes, the entire collection is located in my 'Kiss Room'!

PM: Do you buy tees both mint and love-worn?

JR: Mint condition for any collectible – especially a shirt – is always ideal, but ironically enough, with T-shirts half their character is how they were worn and clearly loved back in the day. Still, the overall quality and level of usage would affect the price of the item dramatically, which could affect my decision to purchase. If it's a really rare shirt in pretty rough condition, I would have to pass, but if it's in great shape overall and worn only a bit, it's probably a shirt I would like to have.

PM: Do you keep your collection to a specific period?

JR: Well, Kiss's golden years from 1976 to 1979 saw the first big boom of their merchandise, more specifically in 1978 when Kiss was the biggest band in America. The original line-up at this time, and the glory period associated with it, is what makes this 'make-up era' of Kiss merchandise worth the most, therefore the most collectible and desirable. The less popular 1980 to 1983 period, which featured a few different line-ups, may be considered less valuable because the band's peak had passed, but some of the merchandise from that period is worth more than something from 1977, only because it was not as mass produced and also in many cases available only overseas, specifically in Australia, from 1980 to 1981. Kiss's second make-up wave, beginning with the record-breaking 1996–1997 Alive/Worldwide Reunion tour, also yielded another round of major merchandising that a lot of people have grown fond of, probably because it reminded them of a time 20 years earlier when Kiss items were everywhere.

PM: Do any of your tees have stories attached to them?

JR: Well, the 1976 to 1977 Rock 'n Roll Over tour shirt I have is one of my favourite – and possibly most rare – ones. It was purchased by my brother at Kiss's first time playing at New York's famous Madison Square Garden, 18 February 1977 [see page 156]. Although I was too young to go to the show – and believe me I wanted to – it was only a few years later that I got the coolest hand-me-down yet. This is truly a vintage shirt from a very famous gig in Kiss's illustrious history.

PM: Which tee is the jewel in your crown?

JR: The 1982 to 1983 Creatures of the Night jersey is probably the most rare shirt I have, because it comes from a tour that was short-lived and also the only one to feature new members Eric Carr and Vinnie Vincent in full make-up and costume. Many major markets were skipped over for this tour, so shirts like this one were sold in much smaller quantities than your average Kiss tour shirt. I also would imagine that the Rock 'n Roll Over shirt I have (the one I inherited from my brother) is quite valuable, not only because of how old it is, but also because of the history of the actual gig and venue where it was purchased.

PM: What do you think about high-end vintage stores that inflate prices of 'fashionable' rock shirts?

JR: I think high-end vintage stores who find old concert tees and sell them for ridiculous prices are only making this market more collectible, in addition to somehow spreading the idea that these could be considered fashionable. If it gives more attention to older bands or somehow breathes new life into a name or logo, then that's pretty cool.

Above and opposite: Kiss in Concert, Alive in '79 tour shirt.

Opposite: Cheap Trick tour shirt, 1980.

Above: Cheap Trick, *In Color* LP advertisement,
Bomp magazine, November 1977.

Above and below: Cheap Trick, Midwest power-pop legends, tour shirt, 1981.

Above and below: Cheap Trick,
US tour shirt, 1979.

Opposite: Cheap Trick in Concert, 1980.

Above and below: Van Halen T-shirt, early 1980s.

Above and opposite: Meat Loaf,
Bat Out of Hell concert shirt, 1978.

Above: ZZ Top, She's Got Legs iron-on shirt, 1984.

Below: ZZ Top, She's Got Legs band shirt, 1984.

Above and below: ZZ Top Eliminator tour jersey shirt,
complete with sleeve print, 1984.

Above and right: Mötley Crüe, Girls, Girls, Girls, 1987.

Opposite: Guns n' Roses shirt featuring artwork for their first LP *Appetite for Destruction*, 1987.

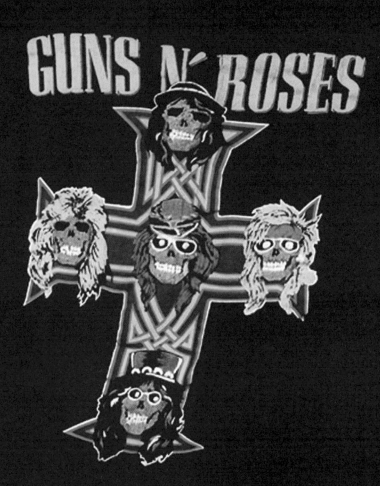

Above: Def Leppard and the Women
of Doom, *Hysteria*-era band shirt, 1987.

Opposite above: The Rolling Stones, promo
shirt for the *Love You Live* album release, 1977.

Opposite below: The Rolling Stones, She's So Cold and I'm
So Hot shirts, depicting the classic tongue logo.

Above and opposite: Bon Jovi, 'You Give
Love a Bad Name' promo shirt, 1986.

Above and opposite: Rod Stewart, Blondes Have More Fun shirt, advertising a three-night showcase concert in New York's Madison Square Garden, June 1979.

Above and below: Billy Joel, Live in NY,
the Ameri-Canada tour, 1980.

Above and below: Bruce Springsteen and the E Street Band,
Born in the US jersey tour shirt, 1984 –1985.

LIVE AID
13 JULY, 1985

In July 1985, as a result of Live Aid, Run the World and Feed the World, more basic white T-shirts were sold in the UK than any year previously. In fact, so many shirts were sold to the supporting public that for the rest of the summer wholesalers were left exhausted and couldn't catch up with the demand.

Opposite: Crowd shot of Live Aid, Wembley Stadium, London, 1985.

Above: Live Aid, The Global Jukebox – This T-Shirt Saves Lives, 1985.

Above and opposite: Live Aid, This Shirt Saves Lives, 1985.

QUEEN

Above: Queen World tour '76, featuring the famous Queen Crest band logo (based on Freddie Mercury's original design), and as seen on the *A Night at the Opera* album cover. This shirt emerged during the Japan and Australia tours of 1976.

Above: Queen's US tour, 1978. This shirt from the October–December tour of 1978 features the *Jazz* album artwork – that which spawned the infamous nude bicycle race around Wimbledon Stadium.

Opposite above: Queen world tour 1978. Queen caused uproar in 1978 with their *Bicycle Race* video and 'Fat Bottomed Girls' song. This shirt, a souvenir from the huge tour, derives from that notorious and unforgettable footage.

Opposite below: Queen's US tour 1976 for *A Night at the Opera*. The Crest logo has inspired countless Queen merchandise items over the years. This rare shirt originates from the US tour that kicked off in January 1976.

Above: Queen tour '75 shirt, featuring the very first Crest logo. This long-forgotten souvenir emerged in 1975 and is thought to be the only surviving example – but Brian's not selling it!

Above: Queen spring tour '78 shirt. Simple, but no less striking, this *News of the World* album artwork-themed shirt originates from the European tour of 1978. The robot is a much-loved and iconic image.

Opposite above: Again a simple image, but a great example of one of the earliest known Queen T-shirts. This promotional item was issued by Elektra Records (in the US) in 1974, and borrows from the artwork of the band's 1973 debut album.

Opposite below: Commemorating Queen's massively successful Works tour of 1984, this shirt features imagery from Fritz Lang's silent classic *Metropolis* – the film featured in Queen's *Radio Ga Ga* video of the same year. Yet another mega-rare item!

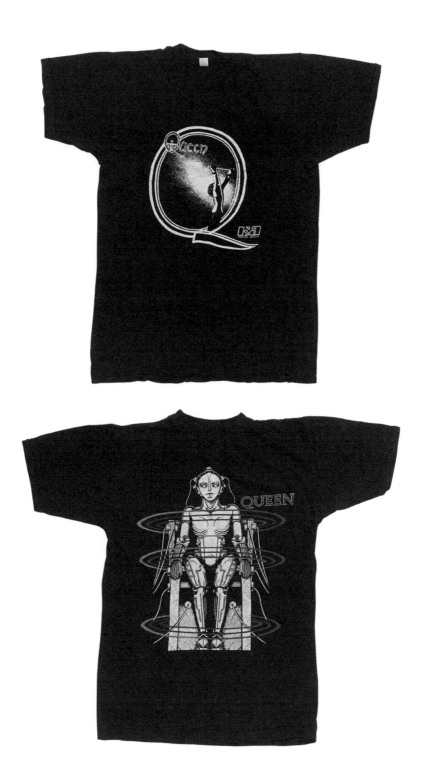

Above and below: Status Quo and Special Guests Live. The 1986 Magic Tour of Europe was one of Queen's biggest and most successful. Status Quo were the support for a number of the UK concerts. The entire tour sold out within hours.

Above and below: Featuring *A Kind of Magic*
album artwork, this shirt, like most of the examples
shown here, is much sought-after by collectors.
The chances of finding one are negligible.

199

80S METAL

Emerging from 1970s heavy rock bands, such as Black Sabbath and Deep Purple, 1980s metal brought a new electrically charged sound to a generation. Drums were loud, lyrics dark, the guitar was heavy and the beat was hard. This high energy resonated with a huge tribe of predominantly male youth searching for a more aggressive, fantastical form of escapism from the everyday grind. Lengthy, indulgent guitar solos were pivotal, as were horror-flick lyrics that took listeners from heaven to hell. The metal crowd had long hair, skinny jeans, high-top trainers, and their band T-shirts were worn tight. Here's a look at the metal mania shirts of the period.

Opposite: An absurd heavy-metal collage T-shirt
of popular metal and rock acts of the day, late 1980s.

Above and opposite: Venom, UK black metal
band, US Invasion tour shirt, 1984.

Above and below: Slayer, Hell Awaits tour shirt, 1985.

Above and below: Slayer, Slatanic Wehrmacht shirt, 1985. The Nazi connection made this shirt a little controversial, but it was also the name of their fan club.

Above: Young Metal Attack shirt, the first-ever
Metallica T-shirt, which was mainly given to band
members and friends, early 1980s.

Opposite above: Metallica, European tour shirt for
…*And Justice for All* album, 1988.

Opposite below: Metallica, Ride the Lightning
world tour shirt, 1984.

Above and below: Metallica, Damage Inc. tour for *Master of Puppets* album, 1986.

Above and below: Metallica, Metal Up Your Ass, 1985. The first-ever version of this shirt, bought at Metallica's debut performance at the Donington Monsters of Rock Festival in the UK.

COLLECTOR

STEVE GILL, STAMFORD, ENGLAND

PM: What attracted you to metal?

SG: A friend of mine passed me a tape at school; it was a metal compilation. I fell in love with it straight away and I got this funny feeling when I heard it – it clicked. Before that I hadn't completely identified with any music specifically. I loved the aggression of it. It was loud, hard and heavy, different and full of energy. It was plugged into the mains. I wanted to find out more and I started collecting vinyl, then shirts.

PM: Your T-shirt collection is top-drawer. Do you wear the tees?

SG: To gigs, I mainly wear tees from the mid 1980s – the fit's right for metal look. The shirts were skinny in the 1980s, tight fit with cap sleeves. I sometimes wear these tees to gigs until they're wrecked, they fall to pieces, then I sew them back together and start again. The shirts got baggier in the 1990s and the shape changed. I still buy them, but they don't have the same skin-tight, metal shape.

PM: Do you buy 'boots' or official only?

SG: I buy official only, no bootlegs. I'll buy bootleg records, but never shirts. I don't collect any modern shirts either – modern meaning the last five years. I buy shirts from every show I go to, but I buy them just to wear, not to collect. When something's five years old, it becomes part of the collection.

PM: What's your best-ever score?

SG: The Young Metal attack shirt, definitely. It's the first Metallica logo T-shirt ever. I swapped for it – I had five or six great shirts from the *Master of Puppets* era, they didn't mean that much to me and a guy I knew was desperate for them. He had a friend who'd known the band from the beginning and he had the first ever Metallica shirt, so we traded. I just had to have it, and when I got it, I loved it.

PM: Are there any tees you could never part with?

SG: I've got a great old *Ride the Lightning* T-shirt that was owned by Scott Ian from Anthrax, so it's like the ultimate metal shirt. And there's a black Doris Pushead T-shirt from 1988 to 1989 that I wore to every show I went to from 1996 to 2004. There's something about that shirt that's full of attitude. I couldn't part with it as the memories from those shows are with the shirt.

PM: Was there a metal shirt you had to really dig around for, that was difficult to get your hands on?

SG: There's a *...And Justice for All* white shirt, 1988 to 1989 that Lars, the drummer, wore in a video on Metallica. I couldn't find it for ages. I had to really hunt around, and then two came up at once, so I got them both. I can wreck one, then start on the next.

Above and opposite: Twisted Sister,
Stay Hungry tour shirt, 1984/1985.

Above and opposite: Slayer, Live Undead, Dead Ahead tour shirt, 1985. This classic Slayer shirt design features the *Live Undead* EP cover artwork on the front and the tour dates for a short West Coast tour on the back.

Above and opposite: Slayer, Haunting the Chapel, 1986.

Redman Productions Presents

DIRTY ROTTEN IMBECILES

D.C.'s
BLACK MARKET BABY

RHYTHM PIGS

Appearing at:
THE COMPLEX

friday jüNe 6

UNDERGROUND

HARDCORE PUNK, THRASH & CROSSOVER

Opposite: Dirty Rotten Imbeciles gig shirt for the Complex venue. This shirt was made for just one show – the Complex in Washington DC, US, in the summer of 1986.

Above: Suicidal Tendencies skate-punk shirt, 1983.

Opposite above: Napalm Death, one of the
first shirts made for the band, 1986/1987.

Opposite below: Cro-Mags, *Age of Quarrel* shirt, 1986.
Not the first Cro-Mags shirt, but the first shirt
that came out on release of the album.

Above: Jody Foster's Army, Californian
skate-punk tour shirt, 1985.

Above: Black Flag, *In My Head* band shirt, 1985

Opposite: Black Flag, *Loose Nut* band shirt, 1985

Opposite and above: Monsters of Rock Metal Madness,
a one-day UK festival featuring an all-star line-up,
including Metallica, Van Halen and Scorpions, 1988.

Above: Crumbsuckers, NY hardcore band,
T-shirt artwork by Sean Taggart, late 1980s.

Above: Accused, Panic in the
Casket tour shirt, late 1980s.

Above and right: Anthrax, classic NOT-man skating design, *Among the Living* era, 1986/1987.

Opposite: Metallica white Doris shirt, designed by Pushead in 1988. This example has been cut down into a vest, but it is believed that the white shirt was released before the black one; they are very hard to find.

Above and opposite: Accused, Martha
Sucks Brains shirt, late 1980s.

JERSEY SHIRTS

Well known in the US, jersey shirts are baseball-style tees with three-quarter-length sleeves. They are most commonly tour shirts and were produced in abundance in the 1970s and 1980s. Nearly always double sided and sometimes even featuring extra sleeve prints, they are probably the most elaborate and decorated of all band shirts. Although mass produced at the time, they now have a cult following among T-shirt collectors. The style was used across all genres of music, from Motörhead to Michael Jackson, though they were particularly favoured by the stadium rock and metal bands of the era.

Above: Black Sabbath, a *Sabbath Bloody Sabbath*-esque bootleg shirt. Back in the 1980s there was a slew of bootleg shirts available outside shows or at flea markets, county fairs, and so on. This is one from that era, but with a unique, noteworthy design.

Above: Venom US tour jersey, 1986, commemorating their 'seven dates of hell' for the *Possessed* album.

Above and below: Kiss jersey-style tour shirt, celebrating and promoting their 10th Anniversary tour, 1983.

Above and below: Judas Priest, Point of Entry tour jersey, 1981. It was on this tour that Iron Maiden opened for them.

Above and opposite: Judas Priest,
Screaming for Vengeance tour shirt, 1983.

Above and below: Kiss band shirt 1979/1980. The front depicts Kiss in full make-up, while the back view shows rare unmasked illustrations. The sleeves have classic Kiss Army logo prints.

Above and below: Black Lace, lesser-known NY girl rock group, tour shirt for the *Unlaced* album, 1984/1985.

Above and opposite: The Rolling Stones,
jersey-style US tour shirt,1981.

Above and opposite: Joan Jett, jersey shirt for her
Bad Reputation album, 1981. Probably not official.

Above and below: Megadeth, Peace Sells… But Who's Buying? tour jersey, 1986. Omid (see pages 254–9) bought this when Megadeth were touring with Dark Angel. 'When I wore this to school the next day (I was in eighth grade), the administration made me turn it inside out because of the back. "Rattle Your God Damn Head" was too much for them, I guess!'

Above and below: Grim Reaper, Hell on Wheels tour shirt, 1987. Grim Reaper were part of a new wave of British heavy metal acts.

Above and below: Slayer, Reign in Blood
shirt from their US tour, 1986/1987.

Above and below: Metallica Doris character, designed by Pushead, 1988.

Above and below: Judas Priest, Defenders of the Faith tour jersey, 1984. This is a specially made, one-off shirt for the Washington, DC, shows, featuring great graphics of the White House and member Rob Halford on the Lincoln Memorial.

Above and below: AC/DC, Fly on the Wall tour jersey
shirt, 1985. The date of the gig the owner saw is highlighted
in black marker on the back of the shirt.

Above and below: Led Zeppelin, jersey-style band shirt, late 1970s.

Above and below: Dokken, Rockin' America tour jersey shirt, 1987.
This shirt came from the show where Dokken were opening for
Twisted Sister, who were on their Come Out and Play tour.

Above: Riot, Restless Breed tour jersey shirt, 1982.
Riot was a classic New York-area hard rock/metal band.

Below and opposite: Accept, Metal Heart tour jersey, 1985,
bought when Accept were opening for Iron Maiden on
the spring leg of their Powerslave tour.

COLLECTOR

OMID, NEW YORK, US,
WWW.RUNAWAYSSECRETS.COM

PM: When did you first get into metal and rock music? Why did it strike a chord with you?

D: I first got into rock music when I was barely out of diapers, if I even was out of diapers! My mom is a big music head and I always credit her with getting me started. I grew up in a house where there was always music playing. I started getting 45s (the Guess Who, Elton John, etc.) back when I was a toddler and had a little toy record player to play them on. My love for the harder rock and heavy metal came in about third or fourth grade when my family moved back to the US [from Iran], I got right into it. I think I was about eight when I got my first Kiss album in 1982. It was *Creatures of the Night*. It probably would have happened earlier if we hadn't moved to Iran for most of the late 1970s. Coming straight from a country where we'd just witnessed a revolution and then a war start, no wonder I was drawn to metal! So I was probably eight years old and found KISS, then got into the rest from there. It was an avalanche that has never stopped.

PM: What's the first music-related tee you can remember buying or being given? How old were you? Was it from a specific concert?

D: Well, the first shirt I got was probably a Kiss iron-on shirt that I remember having to trade my friend in elementary school for some comics or something when we were about nine. I still have it, it's tiny! But the first true concert shirt I got was from Kiss on the Animalize tour, 27 November 1984 at the Baltimore Civic Center when they played with Queensryche. My mom took me – it was three days before my 11th birthday. So yeah, it totally killed, and I bought a shirt at that show and I still have and wear it today. It's the one with the grey sleeves with rings on – it's sort of visible in the picture of my wall of shirts.

PM: Which is the most important tee in your collection, the one with the most personal relevance?

D: Well, the most precious and personal to me is probably my Metallica, Ride the Lightning shirt that I'm wearing in the photo [opposite]. The story goes like this… I was in sixth grade, it was right after my 11th birthday and a girl in my grade had an older brother Ryan, who was a diehard metal head. I remember going to his house and he just had so many great records, posters, shirts, import, crazy stuff that was hard to get back then – you had to really work to find this stuff! So one Sunday, 13 January 1985, I get a call from him out of the blue saying, 'Hey man, there's this show in Maryland this afternoon and we have three tickets, but no ride there – if you can get us up there, you can have the extra ticket.' The show was Metal Massacre 1985 that featured WASP, Metallica and Armored Saint. I have no idea how I managed to get my parents to agree to it, but somehow my mom drove us the 45 minutes up to the club and dropped us off for the show. It was a life-changing experience.

We were so young and small that we couldn't see, so we climbed up and were literally standing inside the PA on the stage, just getting shredded by the volume. It was incredible! Metallica blew me away, but I must admit at the time I was so into WASP that I bought a WASP tour jersey instead of a Metallica shirt.

Ryan, however, bought the Metallica shirt and a couple years later I remember calling him and asking him if he still had it, and if he would sell it to me. I bought the shirt for like $5.

PM: Are you precious with your tees, keeping them wrapped up and in mint condition, or do you wear them day to day?

O: Some of them, like the Runaways ones, I don't wear… they're so delicate now it's not a good idea. The rest, well, I wear them all. I wore the Metallica one I've just talked about for a recent show our band played, which was on the 20th anniversary of the show the T-shirt came from. I am a collector, so I do my best to keep them in good shape, but with shirts I do like to actually wear and share them.

PM: What's your t-shirt want list? Are there any you want, but can't track down, or any you'd die for?

O: Oh, I don't know… there's a few Runaways shirts I don't have that I'd love to find, like the 1977 Japanese tour shirt that looks like Cherie's corset! And they did a red 1976 European tour shirt I've always wanted. But for the most part I'm pretty happy with what I have. I mean, if I see something I like I'll buy it if it's reasonably priced, but I don't really have a list of stuff I'm searching for anymore!

PM: Does it annoy you that 'fashion people' are wearing old rock shirts often without knowledge of the bands or an appreciation of the music, and the crazy prices that shirts can go for in vintage clothing stores in Manhattan?

O: Well, quite honestly, yes. It did bother me for a long time. Sometimes I will still ask some hipster muffin on the streets of NYC if he's really into RATT, but I know the answer is almost always gonna be something that pisses me off, so I have stopped asking. When metal ruled the planet, we bought shirts and wore them because we loved the bands and the music; it wasn't a fashion statement or ironic in anyway. I have never worn a band shirt for any reason other than because I like the band.

I don't really feel the need to get too worked up about this stuff anymore, though. I've already seen it happen once back in the 1980s when the first round of posers came through. There's more important things to worry about. Still, it is kind of annoying … what can I say? As far as the prices, yeah, some of them are crazy, and it's definitely peaking right now. It's just a trend though, it will pass like all trends do, and then the true and the few will still be standing there with their faded concert tees on.

Above: The Runaways Invade Germany T-shirt, 1978. This shirt is believed to have been sourced from someone who worked for the group, and it's probably one of the few authentic Runaways tour shirts.

Above left: The Runaways, Prince of Pop T-shirt, 1975/76. Another iron-on letter shirt, this one was made for the famous scenester and DJ Rodney Bingenheimer who was a big part of the LA scene back at the time, and the subject of the film *Mayor of Sunset Strip* (2003).

Above right: Original Runaways belt, *Waiting for the Night* promotional item, 1977.

PM: Do you think rock/metal peaked in the mid 1980s? What do you think of current stuff? Do you wear modern shirts?

O: Yes, I think that music in general peaked between the mid to late 1960s through to the mid to late 1980s. I feel fortunate to have caught the '80s and always bummed I missed the '60s and '70s. As far as what's happening today, I couldn't care less about most of it. I wear some modern bands, mostly just local bands or friends who I dig and support like Bad Wizard, Villains, Deceased, that kind of stuff. And I wear Battletorn shirts because I like our band. Even though Beverly (our singer) says it's a no-no, I support my own scene – I mean, if I don't like our band enough to wear a shirt, I shouldn't be in the band!

PM: Do you buy up tees because you like the design, whether it fits you or not?

O: Oh yeah, I've bought shirts that are too big, if it's one of a kind and I want to just have it for the stash. But that's pretty rare. As I said, I usually like to be able to wear them. Luckily I'm still able to fit into most of my old shirts.

PM: Do any of your other shirts have stories attached to them?

O: Many of my shirts came from shows I was at, so they all have memories attached. And then there's ones people have given me, which are important, too. They remind me of events, different times, friends… they tell a story of my path.

PM: Your Runaways collection is second to none. What makes you so into them in particular?

O: The Runaways just quite simply rule! I have been asked this question so many times, by so many people, and it's still one I can't elaborate on too much. I like to keep the answer kind of simple. Either you get it or you don't, but I personally feel they were revolutionary and unique in what they did. They just kick ass, good punk/hardrock delivered by hot young ladies – it was a great package. They paved the way for so many other bands.

As far as why I chose them to get so deeply into, again, it was just something I felt I wanted to do and I did it. I'm an extremist, and if I do something it's usually all the way. I collected the Runaways all the way. I've found so much stuff on this band, which amazes me since they were around for less than four years and only released four studio albums and one live one in that time.

PM: Any last words about T-shirts, music or your collection?

O: Thanks for doing this book, it will allow people to see shirts that they may never have seen otherwise. Shirts are an important part of music history, of the whole package and scene, so it's cool that they're being seen as such! And as far as collecting, just have fun with it and try and stay true. By that I mean follow your heart, and not the trends… in music, and in life!

Opposite: The Runaways Crawdaddy T-shirt, 1976. This was a custom-made shirt of the *Crawdaddy* magazine 1976 cover story on the band. There are many pictures of Joan wearing this shirt throughout the 1970s – she crossed out members as they quit.

Above: *And now… the Runaways* sneakers promo item for the album of the same name.

Above: This shirt, from the 1970s, was probably made by a fan for Sandy West of the Runaways.

Below: Not an official Runaways shirt, but one you could order from magazines. Note that Joan Jett is missing from the picture.

Above and below: The Runaways, Golden West Ballroom T-shirt. This shirt that was made by the venue, but has no specific date so it could have been from any of the shows between 1976 and 1978.

Above: The Runaways, *Waiting for the Night* fan-made shirt, 1970s. This one belonged to Joan Jett and looks hand-drawn, but it's a silkscreen.

Below: When the Runaways started in 1975, drummer Sandy West's mother made these shirts with iron-on letters. This was one of Joan's.

Above: The Runaways, Atlanta shirt, 1978. A one-off, probably made by the
venue or promoter – there were very few official tour shirts made.

Below: Joan Jett's Golden West Ballroom shirt, 1976. As band members quit,
she crossed them out or burned off their faces with cigarettes.

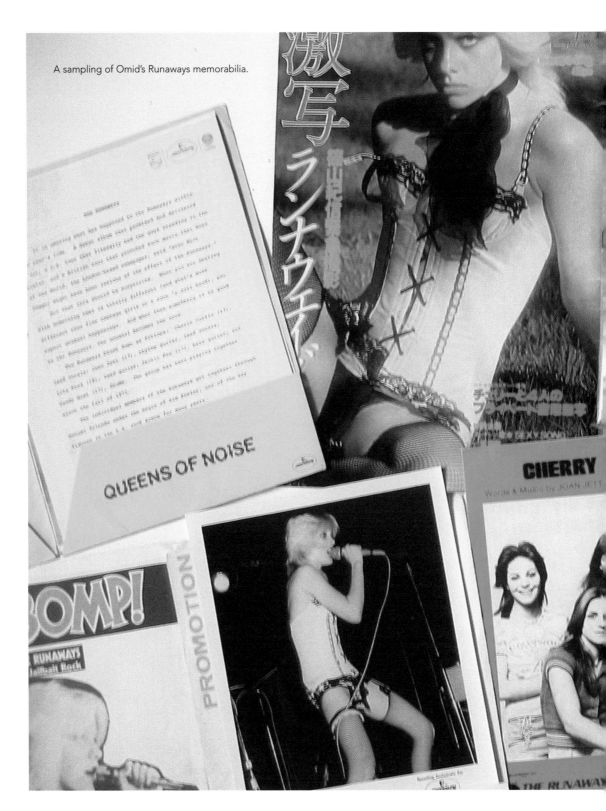

A sampling of Omid's Runaways memorabilia.

PUNK

In the mid 1970s, punk arrived and breathed a breath of fresh air into the otherwise terminally dull decade that was still recovering from an excessive hangover of the excitement of the 1960s. At long last youth was on the rise again as the Pistols and their peers reflected the hopes, dreams, fears and personal politics of the generation. Not since the mid 1960s mod, beat group scene had British youth projected so much raw energy – the kids had temporarily lost their minds in a hippie-fuelled drug haze around 1968. The Sex Pistols, Clash and Ramones need little introduction, and their greatness cannot be denied.

Above: The Sex Pistols line-up, 1977.

Opposite: *The Great Rock 'n' Roll Swindle,* artwork of the posthumous Pistols cash-in flick, 1980.

Above and opposite: I Survived shirt, from the Sex Pistol's first, and last, US tour in 1978. It was most famously worn by drummer Paul Cook in the film *The Great Rock 'n' Roll Swindle*.

430 KINGS RD

They are Dickensian-like urchins who with ragged clothes and pock marked faces roam the streets of foggy gas lit London. Pillaging.

All

Setting FIRE to Buildings BEATING-UP old people with gold chains Fucking the rich up the arse, Causing havoc wherever they go. Some of these ragamuffin gangs jump on TABLES amidst the charred

Let It Rock, Too Fast to Live Too Young to Die, Sex, Seditionaries: a slew of names, but all these incarnations of one small Chelsea, London, shop had several things in common – a peripatetic artist and Dickens-obsessed band manager/manqué called Malcolm McLaren, an ex-primary school teacher by the name of Vivienne Westwood and a desire, not only to be different, but to be seen to be different: loudly, obnoxiously and profitably. From retro teddy boy threads to shirts proudly proclaiming Fuck Your Mother Punk and Don't Run Away, or emblazoned with swastikas, few concepts were taboo in this crucible of punk anarchy that spawned its own house band, the Sex Pistols.

Opposite, above and following pages: The Oliver Twist Manifesto was one of McLaren's last Seditionaries' designs and encapsulated his vision of the Sex Pistols.

and so in 19..
remains the SE...
active Extremism
are at not tec...
WHAT COMM
RIGHT OUT
RY AS
KEEN
possibly, can in

thers sick.
PISTOLS Their
all ~~they~~ they
that's what
to JUMP
the
AST YOU
RY
to CREATE

Above and opposite: This design was an amalgam of an image produced for a Wembley rock 'n roll revival gig and a Molotov cocktail recipe from *The Anarchist Cookbook*, published in 1970.

TIQUARIUS and all it stands for/Michael
x and useless/YES/Leo Sayer/David Essex/
rt oh for money and an audience/Elton J
e Birthday spending/ and shopping/
ROWNS. Take Six, C s bars/Good
t when its really or funny Be
ience/Arse kickers Osborne Harry Pi
n Bragg P Jenkinson The ICA and its
nger Andr David Frost Peter Bog
/The Village Tro rshop (a booksho
po of media caus harmless creativit
ve/THE ARTS COUNCIL of the Metropol
tic foods/Tate & Ly Corrupt councillo
ies/Dirty books that are nt all that
l/Nigel Weym David Hockney and
/The Stock change/Ossie Clark Big
ntiques of sort/Ho ng u
housing/Bianca Jagger John
rthurs/Tramps/Dingwalls without b.
OVIES/Sir Keith Joseph and his
eeches/National Front/W.H. Smith
Chris Welch and his lost Melody

Opposite and above: The first time the Sex Pistols made
it into print, on a shirt co-designed by Bernard Rhodes.
Rhodes later became manager of the Clash.

Above and opposite: An early example of Westwood couture. Pillowcase shirts were made simply by roughly stitching two cotton panels together, leaving apertures for the neck and arms.

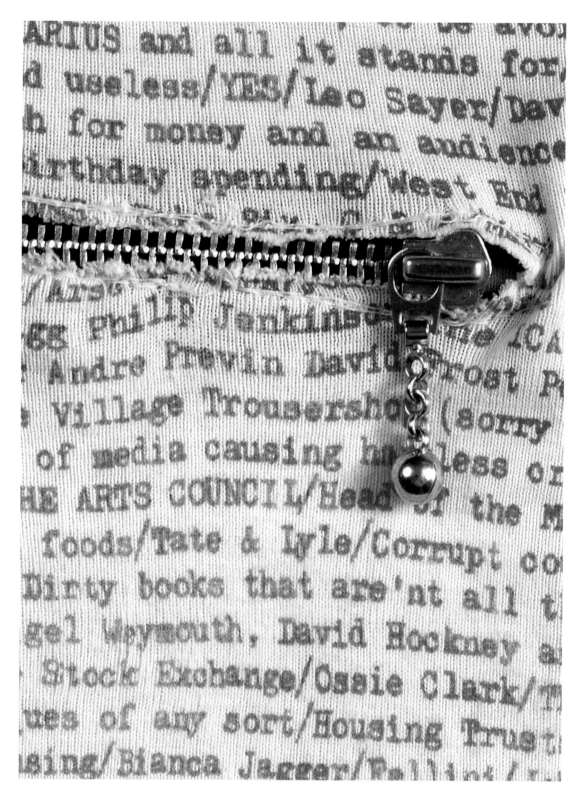

This page and following pages: Artist Jamie Reid adapted an official portrait of Queen Elizabeth II to create several versions of probably the most iconic punk image ever. They were printed on surplus, white Prison Service shirts, pillowcase shirts and bondage shirts manufactured from muslin. The designs caused uproar in 1977, which was Queen Elizabeth's Silver Jubilee year. The shirt shown right once belonged to Joey Ramone.

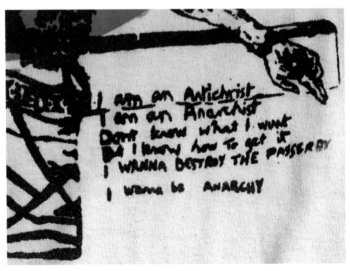

Opposite: Designed to upset the majority of people in one way or another, this shirt remains illegal in Germany.

Above: Images were printed on whatever shirts were cheaply available. Although white cotton was most often used, a range of colour combinations were produced.

Below: The gimp image resulted in the police raiding the shop in their hunt for a serial sex offender active in Cambridgeshire. They did not find him there.

Opposite: A notable example of lack of taboos, the image of a pre-pubescent boy smoking a cigarette was culled from a paedophile magazine. Sex Pistols bassist Glen Matlock hated it.

Above and following pages: Jamie Reid created an irreverent montage from a cut-up Union Jack 'ransom note' lettering and bulldog clips to promote the Sex Pistols' first single.

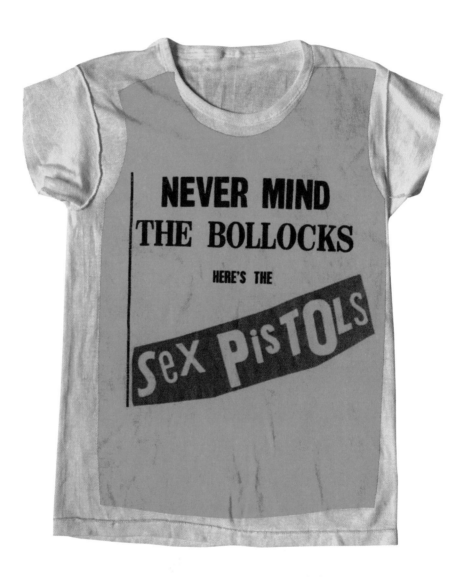

Above and opposite: Warner Brothers modified Jamie Reid's album cover design for American promotional shirts. They followed Westwood's innovation and turned the shirts inside out before screen-printing.

Above and opposite: Ramones shirt, bought on London's Kings Road in 1977. The style of this unofficial shirt is a take on the Seditionaries' designs of the time.

Above: PiL, Public Image Limited, 1979,
ex-Pistols John Lydon's project.

Above: Ramones band shirt, early 1980s.

Above: Unofficial Ramones shirt, late 1970s. Ramones' shirts have been 'booted' to death.

Opposite: The Clash, 1977. An early shirt depicting their first LP cover artwork plus scenes from the Notting Hill riots in London the previous year.

NEW WAVE & BEYOND

Punk rock was the spark for a genuine youth phenomenon. It seemed as if the world had changed almost overnight and that the movement had stirred the imaginations of the kids. As a result new bands, indie labels and magazines emerged from this new wave of inspired talent. This collection of shirts explores some of the resulting underground subgenres that divided, multiplied and followed well into the 1980s.

Opposite: Kapitalist, 1977. A New York record label and home of early punk band Chain Gang.

Above: Stiff Records label, 1977. This broad-minded indie label formed in July 1976, releasing early records by Devo, Ian Dury, Motörhead and Elvis Costello.

Opposite: Max's Kansas City, 1976, the legendary NY music venue.

Above: The Milkshakes, 1981. The band created a truly authentic, early '60s-sounding raw beat, R&B sound and image.

Below: The Milkshakes, 1982. This band from Chatham, Kent, UK was formed by Billy Childish in 1980 from the ashes of the Pop Rivets.

Opposite: Original *BOMP!* T-shirt mail-order
advertisement, featuring Steve Martin, 1977

Above: Logo T-shirt from *BOMP!* magazine, 1977. Originally
called *Who Put the BOMP!,* this 'zine was the brainchild of
Greg Shaw and targeted true rock 'n roll fans. It was the first
magazine to teach readers about 1960s garage punk records
and to document the new wave of punk.

Above: Lou Reed T-shirt, issue one artwork from *Punk* magazine, January 1976. The mag ran in the US for 15 issues until June 1979.

Below: Sire records promo shirt, listing the labels' new wave signings, 1977.

Above: *Sounds*, the now defunct weekly rock newspaper,
T-shirt, 1983. It depicts a drawing by Savage Pencil of the youth
styles of the day – punk, psychobilly, mod, and so on.

Below: Famous logo shirt from *Creem* magazine, mid 1970s.

Above: ESG band shirt, 1981. This was a Bronx-based, sister no-wave quartet.

Below: San Francisco experimental art group, the Residents, Mark of the Mole shirt, 1981.

Above: The Get shirt, DIY post-punk group, 1980.

Below: The Residents, Mole Show tour, October 1982.

Above: Throbbing Gristle, early industrial noise, 1978.

Opposite above: The Residents, 1982. *Santa Dog* was released on their own label, Ralph Records.

Opposite below: The Residents, Coming in October, *Eskimo* album promo shirt, 1979.

Above: The Modern Lovers, Jonathan Richmond's proto-punk outfit, mid 1970s.

Below: Ian Dury and the Blockheads, Blockhead logo shirt, 1978.

Above: The Damned, famous for releasing the first UK punk single, 'New Rose', drum logo shirt, 1977.

Below: Chelsea, early London punk group headed by ex-porn star Gene October, band shirt, 1978.

Above: The Dead Boys band shirt, 1977. A classic Ohio punk band formed from the ashes of Rocket from the Tombs and fronted by Stiv Bators.

Above: Crime, early San Francisco punk band, 1976.

Above: The Stranglers, *Feline* album artwork shirt, 1982.

Above: The Stranglers' last Reading Rock shirt, 1983.

Above: The Stranglers, *Aural Sculpture* album shirt, 1984.

Below: Back shot of the Stranglers' Dramatise Tour shirt, 1988.

Above and below: Bauhaus, 'Bela Lugosi's Dead' 12-inch single promotional shirt from Small Wonder Records, 1979.

Above: Joy Division, Manchester post-punk group,
Unknown Pleasures album artwork shirt, 1979.

Above: Factory Records logo T-shirt, early 1980s.
Founded in Manchester, England, in 1978, signings
included Joy Division and New Order.

Above: New Order's *Movement* album shirt, 1981.

Below: New Order's 'Procession' single artwork shirt, 1981.

Previous page and above: Ciccone Youth, Sonic Youth side project, 1986.

Below: Sonic Youth, experimental rock/ noise group, Sister '87 tour shirt, 1987.

Above and below: Spacemen 3, For All the Fucked-Up Children of this World, 1989.

Above: Acid E, acid-house craze shirt, late 1980s.

Opposite above: The Justified Ancients of MuMu, electronic sampling act that evolved in to the KLF, 1988–1989.

Opposite below: E, Can You Feel It?, late 1980s drug-exploitation shirt.

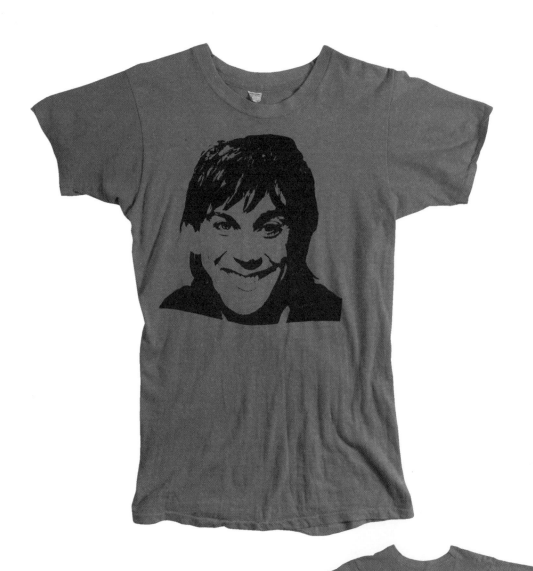

Above and right: Iggy Pop, former Stooges lead man, *Lust for Life* album promo shirt, 1977.

Opposite: Blondie iron-on shirt from 1978. Blondie was the pin-up girl of the 1970s and adorned the walls and T-shirts of countless teenagers.

SUPERSTARS OF THE '70S

The early 1970s saw an emerging generation of young music fans looking for new celebrity personas that they could identify with – artists with a rebellious edge that could offer escapism and excitement to bored teenagers. The following acts offered exactly that. They were musical stylists and visionaries with a theatrical and artistic edge, hugely successful but never middle of the road.

Above: David Bowie world tour shirt, 1978. This brief
tour included music from both *Low* and *Heroes*.

Above: Early to mid 1970s Bowie tee, probably
a bootleg as the design bears little resemblance
to officially released artwork.

Above and below: Lou Reed, Rock & Roll Animal, early 1970s. Solo shirt from the former Velvet Underground frontman.

Right: David Bowie, *Station to Station*-era shirt, 1976.

Opposite: Blondie, Blondie is a Group, from the power-pop *Parallel Lines* period, 1978.

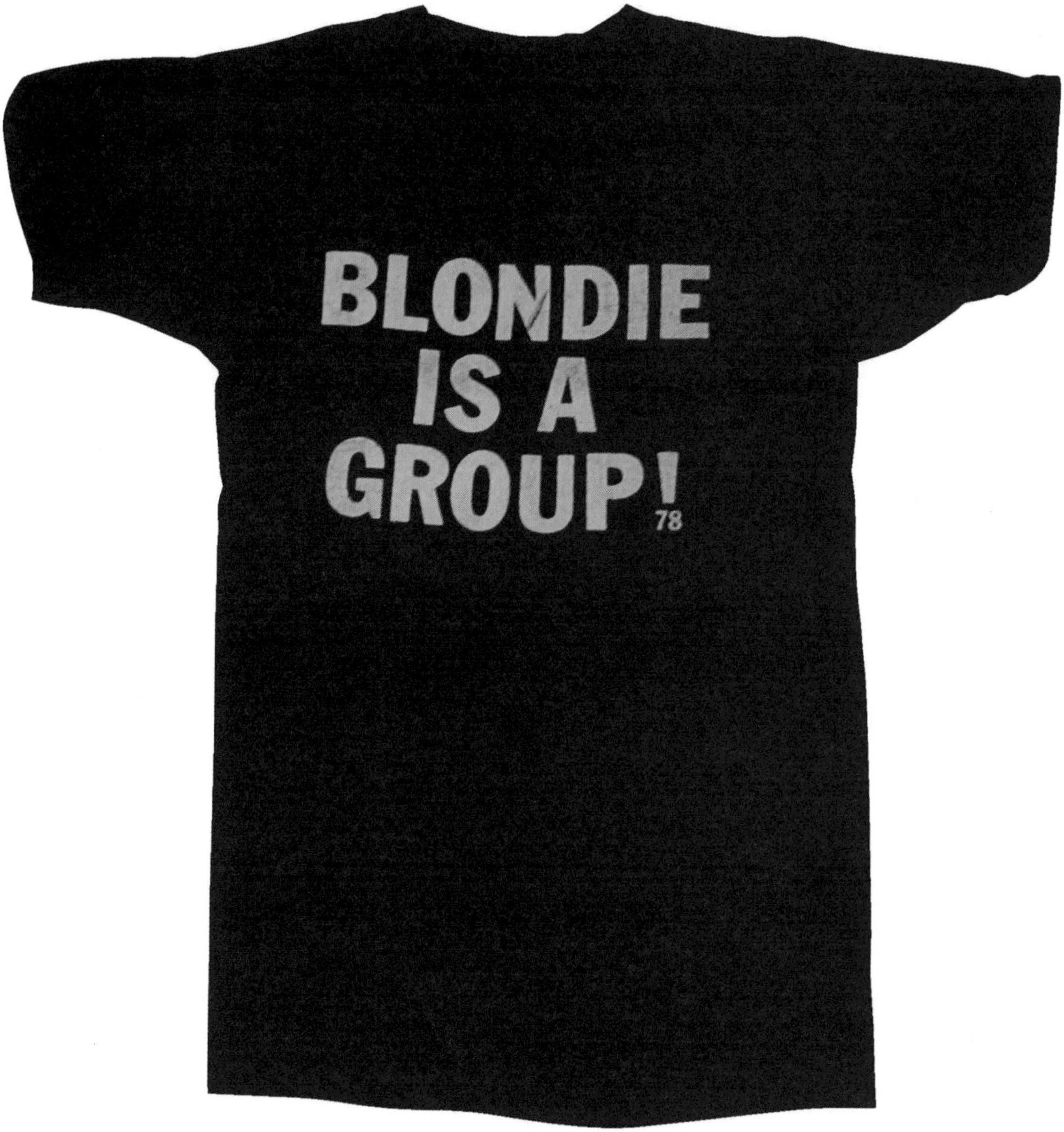
BLONDIE
IS A
GROUP!
78

Above: Blondie, Live in Concert full-colour, iron-on T-shirt, 1980. Probably from the *Autoamerican* period.

Opposite above: David Bowie, 1983. Peculiar print depicting Bowie's changing image, including Ziggy glam rock as well as the *Let's Dance* era.

Opposite above: Bowie photographic iron-on, probably from the *Heroes* or *Lodger* periods, late 1970s.

Above: Brian Ferry, early solo shirt, mid 1970s.

Below: Blondie, shirt from the
Eat to the Beat period, 1979.

Opposite above: David Bowie, Glass Spider
European tour shirt, 1987.

Opposite below: David Bowie, Serious Moonlight
tour shirt, 1983. This was the tour of the hugely
successful *Let's Dance* album.

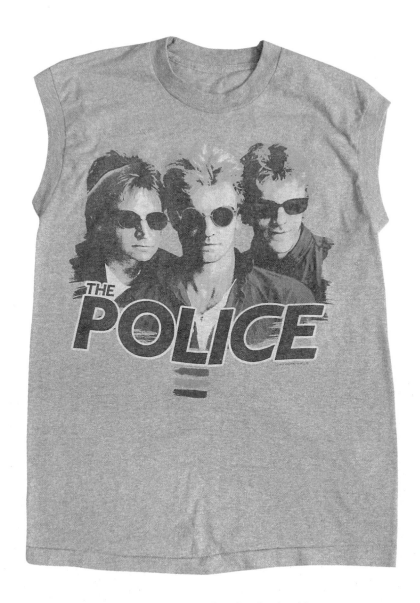

Above and opposite: The Police, Synchronicity
North American tour, 1983–1984.

Above and below: Roxy Music, European tour shirt for their final album, *Avalon*, before the band dissolved, 1982.

Above: Bryan Ferry, *Boys and Girls* solo album shirt, 1985.

Below: Bryan Ferry pin-up shirt, early 1980s.

Above and opposite: Bryan Ferry promo shirt
for the *Solo* and *Roxy* compilation, 1988.

Above: Brian Ferry illustrated
print tee, from early 1980s.

Above: Roxy Music, *For Your Pleasure*
album artwork shirt, late 1970s.

Above and opposite: Blondie, Tracks Across America
jersey tour shirt for the *Hunter* album, 1982.

NEW ROMANCE

A uniquely British scene, the New Romantics emerged in the UK as a reaction to the grim reality of the second wave of UK punk. A pretty broad term as well as a 'movement', New Romantics can be used to conjure up the period of cultural change as the 1980s dawned. It combined the glamour of early 1970s Ziggy-style Bowie with Kraftwork-esque futuristic, synthesized sounds – the guitar became a secondary instrument as the synthesizer and electronics took centre stage. This overtly flamboyant scene saw groups emerge from London club life to high budget, opulent videos and major chart success.

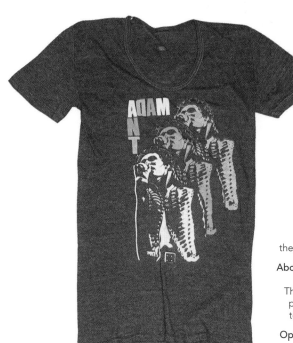

Left: Adam Ant, shirt from the *Stand and Deliver* period, 1981.

Above: Adam and the Ants, *Kings of the Wild Frontier*, 1980. The Ants evolved from art-school punk into New Romantic chart-toppers at the start of the '80s.

Opposite: Gary Numan, UK electro pop pioneer, from the *Pleasure Principle* era, 1979.

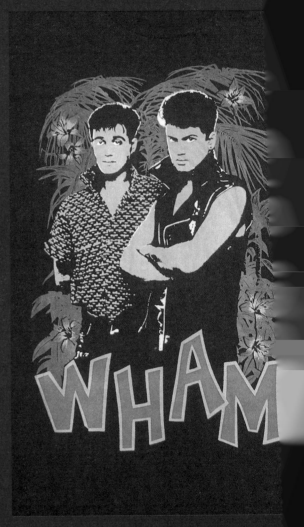

Opposite above left: Teardrop Explodes, Liverpool-based 1980s
psychedelic-tinged group fronted by Julian Cope, 1981–1982

Opposite below left: Culture Club, from the *Colour by Numbers* era, 1983

Opposite right: Wham!, seen by many as the ultimate early 1980s pop group

Above: Nina Hagen, off-the-wall German artist who created a
dissonant mix of punk, funk and opera, 1982–1983

Above: Frankie Goes to Hollywood, Only Frankie Can Stop Me Now, 1984

Opposite above: Ultravox, from the *Systems of Romance* era, 1978

Opposite below left: Soft Cell, synthesizer duo, 1981

Opposite below right: Echo and the Bunnymen, iron-on shirt, early 1980s

Above: Bananarama, fun-filled 1980s
pop girl group, early 1980s.

Below: The Human League, the ultimate
1980s synth pop band, 1981.

Above: Eurythmics, 1983.

Below: Adam and the Ants,
Prince Charming period, 1981.

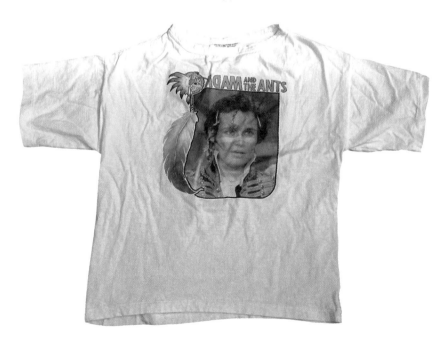

Above: Wham!, iron-on T-shirt, 1982–1983.

Above: Illustrated iron-on of John Taylor,
Duran Duran pin-up, early 1980s.

Above: Duran Duran frontman Simon Le Bon
in *Rio*-style graphics, 1982/1983.

Opposite: Duran Duran, Coca-Cola-sponsored
US tour, featuring the band's first major stadium
dates in America, 1984.

Above and opposite: Duran Duran,
Reflex period US tour shirt, 1984.

'80S MEGASTARS

During the 1980s, three solo artists in particular made the rapid ascent to global superstar status. Madonna, Prince and Michael Jackson became more than musicians, solo artists or teen idols – they created a new level of megastardom, becoming extravagant style icons with an almost super-hero-like appeal. The launch of *MTV* in 1983 fuelled these years of image revolution and proved to be the perfect vehicle for transmitting their flamboyant characters directly into peoples homes, selling their music through groundbreaking cinematic-style videos.

Above: Teen wearing Italians Do It Better shirt from
Madonna's *Papa Don't Preach* video

Opposite: Michael Jackson,
Thriller album promo shirt, 1982.

Above: Michael Jackson, *Thriller* T-shirt, 1982.

Below: Michael Jackson, 'Billie Jean' video-style illustration, 1984.

Above: Michael Jackson,
Thriller full-photo iron-on, 1982.

Below: Michael Jackson, sleeveless T-shirt, 1982.

Above and opposite: Michael Jackson,
unique 'Billie Jean' jersey shirt, 1983.

Opposite: Prince, 'When Doves Cry' single promo shirt, 1984.

Above and below: Prince and the Revolution, 'Kiss' single from the *Parade* album, 1986.

Right: Prince, *Purple Rain* album T-shirt, 1984.

Opposite: Madonna, UK Live transfer shirt, 1987.

Above and below: Madonna, the Virgin tour, 1985.

Opposite: Madonna, *True Blue* album artwork shirt, 1986.

Above and below: Madonna, the Virgin tour picture-disc print, 1985.

Above and opposite: Madonna, world tour T-shirt, 1987. The *Who's That Girl* album was the soundtrack to the movie of the same name starring Madonna. Featuring four Madonna tracks, the album also included Club Nouveau and Scritti Politti.

Above: Madonna, Who's That Girl world tour shirt, 1987.

Below: Madonna, Who's That Girl world tour vest, 1987.

Above: Madonna, Who's That Girl world tour shirt, 1987.

Below: Madonna, Who's That Girl world tour shirt, 1987.

Above: Madonna, early shirt from her first album, 1983.

Above: Madonna, Strike a Pose illustration, late 1980s.

Above: Madonna, early illustration transfer from the 'Lucky Star'/'Borderline' phase, 1983–1984.

Opposite: Madonna, 'Papa Don't Preach' shirt, 1986.

Above: Madonna, Italians Do It Better slogan shirt as worn in the *Papa Don't Preach* video, 1986.

Above: Madonna, Who's That Girl world tour shirt, 1987.

Opposite: Madonna, 'La Isla Bonita' shirt, bought in
1987 from a show at Le Parc de Sceaux, France.

Above: Madonna, Who's That Girl
world tour shirt, 1987.

MADONNA COLLECTORS

WAYNE STANDALOFT
NEW YORK, US

W: I began my Madonna collection in 1984, after seeing the *Lucky Star* video on a Saturday afternoon on *The Chart Show* in England... I was mesmerized, my Mum was calling me and because there was no response on my part she came to find sitting on the floor eyes wide oblivious to the outside world watching Madonna move... I was only six years old!

LK: When did you fall for her completely?

W: The one song which really hooked me onto Madonna is 'Papa Don't Preach' from 1986, the violins at the beginning, the beat, the sound of her voice in the song... and then the video...WOW! That really got me into collector mode. Every picture I would find I would cut out. To this day I have every picture no matter how small and beaten up they are from years of being on my bedroom wall. Now they are in folders and portfolios.

LK: Which T-shirt means the most to you, has the most relevance?

W: I have been to every Madonna tour from the Whose that Girl at Wembley Stadium 1987 on August 18th. I was 10 years old, my first concert ever!! My dad surprised me one day. I was begging for tickets, but my parents said I was too young. Then on August 18th my Dad took me for a drive. We ended up at Wembley Stadium. He said "here you go Wayne," he handed me 2 tickets to see Madonna. I was speechless. 80,000 people there that day. My dad put me on his shoulders and worked his way to the front of the standing area. For the next six hours I was on my dads shoulders... to this day he is still in pain! My dad is one in a million. I got most of the Who's That Girl t shirts at the show. My favourite is the T-shirt with only her eyes.

KELLY SMITH
VIRGINIA, US (BELOW)

I've been a Madonna fanatic since 1983. I first heard Madonna's single 'Holiday' in 1983 and thought, 'Who is that girl?' And recently I met her! I won a contest through *Icon* magazine; I got an invitation to the Bergdorf Goodman/UNICEF party that Madonna hosted. It was a dream come true. I have a picture that was taken of Madonna and me sitting there on the couch, chatting away. The whole thing was so surreal; it was like being Cinderella going to the ball. Madonna is breathtaking. My first words to Madonna were, 'I've been a fan of yours for 20 years.'

FRED GILLOTTEAU
PARIS, FRANCE (OPPOSITE)

I started collecting in 1985. At the beginning I bought magazines and singles, but my first T-shirt was the 'La Isla Bonita' shirt. Madonna has incredible willpower, she wants to be the best, every time, and I like that. When the Re-Invention tour was in France, it was in Paris for four nights, from 1 to 5 September, 2004. The first night I actually had eye contact with her. Finally, at the end of the song 'Crazy for You', she threw her T-shirt in my direction and I caught it – it was fantastic, like a present for my 20 years of support.

DEF JAM

Seminal record label Def Jam came about in 1984 and was founded by producers Rick Rubin and Russell Simmons. Label signings included Public Enemy, Run DMC and the Beastie Boys. The commercial explosion of this label in the mid to late 1980s brought hip hop to a much wider multicultural audience and into the realms of the mainstream. The slick logos from this time were the target of countless bootleggers in the boom years. No black item of clothing was safe, as the simple white logos were emblazoned across almost any garment available.

Above: Beastie Boys, *Licensed to Ill*
album promo shirt, 1986.

Opposite: Beastie Boys, iron-on shirt, 1986.

Above and below: Enemy logo shirt, late 1980s.
The seminal hip-hop group Public Enemy was
formed in New York in 1982.

Above and below: Public Enemy,
classic logo shirt, late 1980s.

Above and below: Public Enemy logo shirt, late 1980s. The instantly iconic logo was designed by Chuck D and depicts E Love (LL Cool J's sidekick) in the sights of a high-power rifle.

Above and below: Public Enemy band shot,
all-over print tee, late 1980s.

Above: Def Jam Recordings,
record label logo shirt, 1986.

Opposite: Beastie Boys, Get Off My....
band logo T-shirt, 1986.

Opposite above: Beastie Boys, transfer-print shirt
with newspaper clippings about their bad behaviour
during their first UK tour, 1986/1987.

Opposite below: Beastie Boys T-shirt featuring
artwork from their first LP gatefold, 1986.

Above: Run DMC Adidas sponsorship shirt,
'My Adidas' *Raising Hell* period, 1986.

CHAPTER 3

POP CULTURE

TV & FILM

Major blockbusters and smash-hit TV shows produce cult characters, heart-throb pin-ups and screen icons, creating an audience of fans desperate to become part of the story and surrounding hype. Kids, in particular, want the story to continue after the show and like to feel that they are part of the action.

Promotional shirts attached to television series and motion-picture productions cash in on the fevered hype of a film's release or a show's high ratings. They experience a density of sales in a normally brief amount of time, as it is often only a matter of months before the next big craze takes over and the once most desired shirt moves to the bottom of the heap.

Above: *E.T.* Phone Home, jersey-style promotional tee, 1982.

Opposite: *E.T., the Extra-Terrestrial*, official Universal Studios poster artwork iron-on shirt, 1982.

E.T.™

PHOTO-LITE 310-0455

© 1982 UNIVERSAL CITY STUDIOS, INC. ALL RIGHTS RESERVED

Opposite above: *E.T.*, Steven Spielberg's cult sci-fi friendly-alien blockbuster, promo iron-on shirt, 1982.

Opposite below: *E.T.* portrait, official promotional iron-on, 1982.

Above: Atari computer game, released 1983. *Star Wars* became much more than a film.

Above: Poster artwork iron-on, *The Empire Strikes Back*,
second instalment of the original trilogy, 1980.

Below: R2-D2, Astromech Droid glitter
iron-on promoting *Star Wars*, 1977.

Above: Official promotional *Star Wars* iron-on, starring C3PO and R2-D2, 1977. Written by George Lucas, this was the ultimate science-fiction fantasy.

Below: *Superman*, seen here as his alter ego Clark Kent, starring Christopher Reeves, 1978.

Above: *Rocky* pin-up iron-on shirt, Sylvester Stallone
as Rocky Balboa, the Italian Stallion, 1976.

Below: T-shirt featuring Sylvester Stallone as the
'one-man army' hero Rambo, *Rambo: First Blood II*, 1985.

Above: Film logo shirt for *Top Gun*, high-flying action flick with Tom Cruise, 1986.

Below: Sylvester Stallone, big-screen action hero pin-up, 1984–1985.

Above: Official poster-art ringer shirt for the monster shark-attack Spielberg classic *Jaws*, 1975.

Above: Original poster-artwork T-shirt for bored-housewife,
mistaken-identity adventure *Desperately Seeking Susan*,
starring Madonna and Rosanna Arquette, 1985.

Above: *Who's That Girl* T-shirt, teenage comedy
flick featuring Madonna as an ex-con out to prove
her innocence, 1987.

Below: Shirt originating from the 1980 film *Flash Gordon*,
with soundtrack and subsequent album by Queen (the
'Flash' single written by Brian May). Freddie Mercury wears
this shirt in the band's *Play the Game* video, 1980.

Above and below: Rare promotional shirt for the cast and crew of *Merry Christmas Mr Lawrence*, tense Second World War prisoner-of-war drama starring David Bowie, directed by Nagisa Oshima, 1983.

Above: *Grease*, summer of '58, high-school musical, with John Travolta as lead Danny Zuco in this pin-up, iron-on, blue marl ringer, 1978.

Above: Unofficial movie cash-in tee featuring
John Travolta, *Saturday Night Fever*, 1977.

Above: Official General Lee glitter iron-on,
Dukes of Hazzard, hit redneck comedy show, 1979.

Above: General Lee *Dukes of Hazzard*
jersey tee, 1979.

Above: Travolta for president, pin-up iron-on from the ABC TV show *Welcome Back, Kotter* period, mid 1970s.

Below: Official *Grease* film poster-artwork iron-on, 1978.

Above: Henry Winkler, aka the Fonze, from American
1950s sitcom 'Happy Days', mid 1970s.

Below: Fonzie for President Ayyy!!,
Arthur Fonzarelli pin-up iron-on, 1976.

Above: You Crazy Fool shirt, featuring Mr T
(B A Barakus) from *The A-Team*, ex-army
commandos action/adventure TV show, 1983.

Above: Official promo *Knight Rider* iron-on; David
Hasselhoff as a modern-day knight with his talking car
Kitt in the adventure TV smash, mid 1980s.

Above: *Miami Vice* iron-on pink T-shirt, from the stylish undercover cop TV show starring Don Johnson, 1985.

Above: Don Johnson pin-up shirt, *Miami Vice*, 1985.

Above: *The Legend of the Lone Ranger,*
ill-fated Western remake shirt, 1981.

Above: Nano Nano glitter iron-on, *Mork and Mindy*, loveable Martian sitcom starring Robin Williams, 1979.

Above: *Fame* shirt, from the 1980 big-screen, teenage stage-school musical.

Above: *Flashdance* shirt, from the
cult 1983 dance/romance chick flick.

Opposite and above: *MTV*'s first annual
video music awards, 14 September 1984.

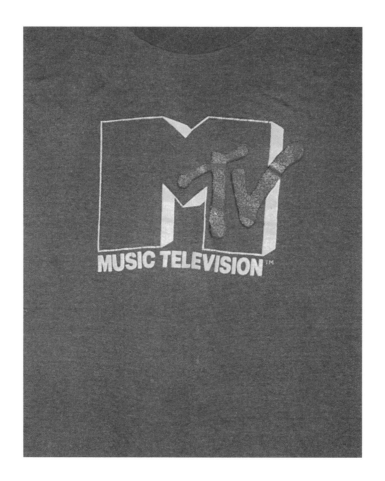

Opposite and above: Music Television: You'll Never
Look at Music the Same Way Again, 1983 /1984.

You'll Never
Look At Music
The Same
Way Again.

COLLECTOR

ANDERS ERIKSEN, NAKSKOV, DENMARK,
WWW.NIGHTMAREGLOVES.COM

PM: Wow, your *Nightmare* collection is off the wall. When did you first discover Freddy?

AE: I heard about *Nightmare 3* when it was showing in the local movie theatre. That must have been late 1987, and I couldn't have been older than 12, but I remember my friends telling me about this incredible film that I just had to see. When they described the scenes and the character of Freddy, I knew I had to check it out.

PM: Can you choose a favourite Freddy/*Nightmare* film?

AE: That's a tough question. I think the original *A Nightmare on Elm Street* and *Wes Craven's New Nightmare* are my two favourites. And if I had to choose one, it would probably be the first, for starting the whole series. Those two movies are both extremely innovative and groundbreaking – they both changed the genre when they were released. Some of the other movies in the series I like especially for specific scenes, but those two have a wholesome quality to them – their imaginative, gripping storylines make them work.

PM: Are you a lover of all things horror or just *Nightmare*?

AE: I'm a huge fan of horror films in general and I collect masks, puppets and props based on other movie monsters, but it's only when it comes to the *Nightmare* memorabilia that I see myself as a serious collector.

PM: The glove you're wearing in your photo looks just like the one from the film.

AE: Thank you. Yes, I've been making gloves for almost ten years now. I make replicas of almost all the gloves that are being used in the films, and I keep adding new items to my website. I've been lucky enough to have both Nancy and Robert Englund [the actor who played Freddy] help me out with my glove business.

PM: What was the first *Nightmare* memorabilia you bought?

AE: My very first purchase was probably the Freddy mask, the screaming model kit and the plastic glove. I had to order these from the US, which wasn't as easy then as it is today.

PM: Which items do you treasure most?

AE: I think I have quite a few items that are really rare, like screen-used pieces, promotional items, etc. But what I really treasure are some of the items that the Englunds have personally sent to me. I also had one of my very first gloves signed by Robert – this still hangs proudly on my wall. I am quite proud of these – not so much because they are rare, but because they define a special time and because some special memories are attached to them.

PM: Which was the first T-shirt you collected? Do you wear the T-shirts or keep them neatly folded away to preserve them?

AE: My first was the Fuck Batman – Here Comes Freddy T-shirt. I wore it, but today almost every *Nightmare* shirt I buy is for the collection only. Sometimes I buy two – one to wear and one for the collection.

PM: Is there anything your collection is missing that you would kill to have?

AE: A screen-used glove. It's ironic that I make them, but I have yet to own a glove that was actually used in a movie.

PM: Where do you find things for your collection?

AE: Everywhere – eBay is a good but expensive place to find interesting things. I've been lucky to get in touch with some people who had interesting *Nightmare* items in store, and who didn't charge an arm and a leg for it. Because of my genuine interest, some people sell items to me for less than they would normally, as they know my intentions aren't to sell them on, but that I really do treasure every item I own.

PM: Have you ever met Robert Englund?

AE: I've had the pleasure of meeting him a number of times, and I think I've got to know him quite well. He is very charismatic, energetic, and he has an incredible knowledge of just about anything. At the same time as being an international horror icon and movie star, he is also a really down-to-earth person, who is in touch with his fans as well as his career. Robert and Nancy are both very artistic, creative and imaginative people, and they have both done much more than I could ever have expected when I first met them. They are very cool people.

Above: Fuck Batman, Here Comes Freddy, 1989.
This unofficial shirt, bought from a souvenir
shop in Copenhagen, was released to coincide
with Tim Burton's *Batman* movie.

PM: Your Freddy room is truly amazing, inspiring and, for me, terrifying – I still have nightmares about the scene where Freddy's tongue comes through the phone even though I saw the film over 15 years ago!

AE: I get new pieces all the time, new items are added almost every week. A dream of mine is to open a *Nightmare* museum one day, where I can have all items displayed like they deserve to be.

PM: Do you buy, sell and trade vintage horror memorabilia or just buy for your collection?

AE: I rarely trade – once it's in my collection it stays there, but I've made *Nightmare* gloves in trade for a unique item. Recently, I did a rather extensive trade with Henry Alvarez for some very special casts of Robert Englund, both in and out of makeup. Most of my 'vintage' items are from the mid 1980s, when the first *Nightmare* film was released. The only earlier items I have are a few original posters from different horror films. So if anyone out there has anything they think I might be interested in, shoot me an email!

Opposite above: *A Nightmare on Elm Street 5: The Dream Child* T-shirt, from the New Line Cinema's fan club catalogue, 1989.

Opposite below left: Early *A Nightmare on Elm Street* T-shirt, 1985.

Opposite below right: *A Nightmare on Elm Street*, Freddy Krueger Bad Boys fan club T-shirt, originally sold with matching Freddy shorts, 1988.

Following pages: Anders' stupendous *Nightmare* memorabilia.

Above and opposite: *A Nightmare on Elm Street 4: The Dream Master,* Wanna Suck Face? promo shirt, 1988.

Above: *A Nightmare on Elm Street 3:
Dream Warriors* promo shirt, 1987/1988.

Below: *A Nightmare on Elm Street 4:
The Dream Master* promo shirt, 1984.

Above and below: *A Nightmare on Elm Street 5, Don't Dream and Drive* promo shirt from the Freddy fan club, 1989.

Above and opposite: *A Nightmare on Elm Street 5: The Dream Child*, stripe-printed shirt, 1989.

COMICS & CARTOONS

Promotional cartoon and comic shirts aren't just for kids. For decades, rock stars and style icons alike have been wearing cartoon characters on their tees as fashion items, and they continue to do so. Original Snoopy and Mickey T-shirts are endlessly desirable in the vintage trade, as these characters have become icons to be worn in their own right. From Snoopy to Catwoman, Miss Piggy to the Hulk, feast your eyes on what are, without doubt, some of the greatest examples of popular art and design classics of the twentieth century – which is even more amazing considering that a few were first penned as early as the 1930s.

Above: Lucy, the know-it-all girl from the gang, mid 1970s.

Opposite: Snoopy sweatshirt jogging
advertisement, mid to late 1960s.

PEANUTS SWEATSHIRT DRESSES . . . Buyers at the spring shows have ecstatical-
ly endorsed our new collection of PEANUTS SWEATSHIRT DRESSES . . . they
come in outrageously bright oranges, blues, yellows, shocking pinks with hysteri-
cally funny Peanuts cartoons and captions. "Surf's Up!" and "To live is to dance
. . . to dance is to live" with Snoopy; Also, "Love is walking hand in hand".

PEANUTS SWEATSHIRTS . . . "Best sellers" to the school set, PEANUTS SWEAT-
SHIRTS designs have been expanded to include Snoopy "Surf's Up" and Charlie
Brown as a dejected baseball manager. Popular with boys, girls, men, women
. . . my grandmother wears one to the market!

DETERMINED PRODUCTIONS, INC.

P.O. Box 2150   **San Francisco, California 94126**

Opposite: Peanuts apparel and sleepwear advertisement, mid to late 1960s.

Above: Snoopy, Let's Jog T-shirt featuring Woodstock, early 1970s. The first Peanuts apparel sweatshirt was printed in 1966, with the range growing from shirts to sleepwear.

Right: Snoopy, It's True… I am a Handsome Dog!, mid to late 1970s.

Below: Snoopy, Chicks Go for Joggers, Champion shirt, early to mid 1980s.

Above: Kansas City baseball-playing Snoopy and Woodstock shirt by Artex (common for original Snoopy shirts), early

Below: Snoopy Doghouse grey marl shirt, early 1980s.

Opposite: Happiness Is Being One of the Gang shirt, featuring Charlie Brown, Sally, Peppermint Patty, Lucy, Linus, Snoopy and Woodstock, mid 1970s. Created by artist Charles Schulz, the Peanuts' characters debuted in 1950.

Opposite: Blondie gives Popeye sex appeal, mid 1970s.

Above: The spinach-eating, bicep-busting Popeye the Sailor Man on a long-sleeve shirt, 1980.

Above: Popeye glitter iron-on, 1979.

Opposite above: Popeye, jersey-style tee, 1982.

Opposite below: Popeye the Sailor Man,
short-sleeve jersey shirt, 1980.

Above: Miss Piggy from *The Muppets* in
a Penn State University cheerleader outfit,
Champion shirt, late 1970s.

Above: Ernie from *Sesame Street*
on a kids' shirt, mid 1970s.

Opposite above: Pink Panther glitter
iron-on, ringer shirt, 1978.

Opposite below: Pink Panther In New York City,
glitter iron-on, Champion shirt, 1978.

Above: Beano and the Bash Street Kids, 1976.

Above: Smurfs playing Pac-man 1981

Below: Bugs Bunny, What's Up Doc, Warner Brothers, 1977

Opposite above: Donald Duck, Walt Disney, late 1970s

Opposite below: Backpacking Mickey, late 1970s

© WALT DISNEY PRODUCTIONS

Opposite above: Goofy, Walt Disney, late 1970s

Opposite below: Super Smurf, artist Pierre Culliford, 1982

Above: Love and Smurfs, early 1980s.

Below: Winnie the Pooh, Walt Disney, early 1980s

Above: *The Catwoman* ringer shirt, mid 1970s.
Originally illustrated by artist Bob Kane, Catwoman first
appeared in 1940 for the first issue of Batman.

Below: *Batman* iron-on, mid 1970s. The caped crusader, DC Comics'
superhero, was originally penned in 1939 by artist Bob Kane.

Opposite: *Spider-Man* cover artwork T-shirt, 1980. Co-created by comic
book artist Steve Ditko and writer Stan Lee, Spider-Man first appeared in
the comic book series *Amazing Fantasy* in 1962.

Above: *The Incredible Hulk* shirt, 1973.
Marvel comic character, created by Stan Lee,
first illustrated by Jack Kirby in 1962.

Top left: Superman, 1970s. *The DC Comics'* superhero first appeared in *Action Comics*, issue 1, June 1938.

Top right: Captain America vest, mid 1970s. *Marvel Comics'* patriotic superhero and leader of the Avengers (the *Marvel* superhero team) was created by artists Joe Simon and Jack Kirby in 1941.

Left: Aquaman, *DC Comics'* undersea hero, early to mid 1970s. The character's first comic book appearance was in 1941.

Right: Wonder Woman ringer-style Champion shirt, mid 1970s. *DC Comics'* creation is cartoons' most iconic superheroine and an ultimate feminist character. She was created by William Moulton Marston in 1941.

Top left: Hulk iron-on jersey baseball-style T-shirt, mid 1970s.

Top right: *The Amazing Spider-Man* vest-style tee, 1981.

Left: Batgirl printed T-shirt, mid 1970s.
The *DC Comics'* superhero first appeared in the
Batman comic, issue 139, April 1961.

Right: *Tarzan, Lord of the Jungle*, iron-on, 1975. The character
was created by Edgar Rice Burroughs in 1914.

Above: Tharg the Mighty, a character from
British sci-fi comic *2000 AD*, early 1980s.

Opposite: Mickey's not just for kids. Johnny Ramone, guitar hero, wearing classic western Mickey Mouse printed T-shirt, late 1970s.

Above, top and right: M. Mouse jersey-style shirt, early 1980s. Mickey Mouse, created in the 1920s by Walt Disney, is arguably the most requested style of vintage tee. The Mickey shirt never goes out of fashion.

Above left: Deadstock Mickey ringer in original shrink seal, early 1980s.

Above: Gun-toting Western Mickey T-shirt,
early 1970s, as he appeared in the 1934
Disney short *Two Gun Mickey*.

Opposite: Variations of the most recognizable
Mickey print, early 1970s to late 1980s.

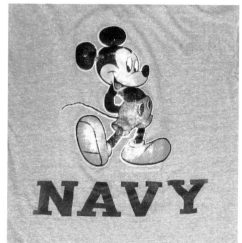

ADVERTISING

Companies were quick to realize the 'walking billboard' power of the T-shirt. Although the earliest promotional shirts were distributed as gifts, it soon became clear that customers would happily pay to display their brand loyalties. Proudly wearing your favourite brand on your chest was the ultimate pledge of allegiance. These shirts were incredibly successful marketing tools as the company would make money on sales and receive free advertising in the process. Used to promote everything from presidential campaigns and fast-food chains to cigarettes and alcohol, there's no limits to the advertising potential of the basic tee. Well-designed trademarks and logos maketh the brand when it comes to these shirts.

Above left: White Castle, I Buy 'Em by the Sack, ringer tee, late 1970s. White Castle (aka the Porcelain Palace) is the oldest American burger fast-food chain.

Above right: White Castle, A Legend in a Bun, white ringer tee, late 1970s. White Castle is famous for their square-shaped slyder burgers.

Opposite: Reese's Pieces sweets, *E.T.* endorsement advertising shirt, 1982.

Opposite: Tassen, unique chequerboard promo tee, early 1980s.

Top left: Marlboro cigarettes promo tee, late 1970s.

Top right: Have fun with People, newspaper promo shirt, early 1980s.

Above left: Dr Pepper, I'm a Pepper advertising tee, mid 1980s.

Above right: Pepsi-Cola advertising T-shirt, 1978.

Above: Max Headroom – Coca-Cola endorsement shirt,
C-C-C Catch the Wave, 1986/1987.

Below: Life Savers sweets, iron-on shirt, 1977.

Above: Martini advertising iron-on, late 1970s.

Below: Kodak centennial anniversary tee, 1980.

Above: Camel Filters cigarettes T-shirt, early 1980s.

Below: Crazy Eddie, US electrical chain, early 1980s.

Above: *CKOM*, Saskatoon Canadian radio station,
T-shirt advertising Rocktober, 1981.

Below: Promo shirt for cult fantasy rock tribute book *Rock Dreams* by artist Guy Peellaert and author Nik Cohn, 1973.

Above: Playboy-esque Mercedes advertising shirt, late 1970s.

Right: Stroh's beer, US brewery company, Detroit, Michigan, 1975.

Below: Shirt advertising Star Dillos, the Eighth International Armadillo Confab and Exposition, in Victoria, Texas, late 1970s.

Above: A glamorous Mediterranean
advertisement for Martini, late 1970s.

Above: Black & White scotch whisky promo shirt, mid 1970s.

Below: Campari aperitif advertising iron-on, mid 1970s.

Above: Blue Ribbon beer by Pabst brewing company, advertising iron-on, mid 1970s.

Below: Budweiser, the King of Beers, cartoon-hero advertisement, mid 1970s.

Above: *Playgirl* magazine, sleeveless T-shirt with classic bunny logo print, early 1980s.

Below: *Playboy* magazine, grey marl T-shirt with flocked iconic bunny logo, late 1970s.

Above: Actifed T-shirt, 1970s. Actifed cold medicine had been famously used by NASA astronaut Wally Schirra to treat a cold on the Apollo 7 mission.

Below: Rat guitar-effect pedals, Stomp on a Rat advertising T-shirt, early 1980s.

Above: US presidential campaign T-shirt, Carter for President, 1976.

Below: Spitting Image-style Margaret Thatcher iron-on shirt, mid 1980s.

Above: Nixon in '88, He's Tanned, He's Rested, He's Ready, tee by Sneakers, 1988.

Below: Comic-style superhero Nixon on blue marl ringer, early 1970s.

MCDONALD'S

Dick and Mac McDonald opened the first McDonald's drive-thru restaurant in San Bernardino, California, in December 1948. The first Ray Kroc franchised McDonald's restaurant opened in Des Plaines, Illinois, on 15 April 1955 (today's McDonald's). The McDonald's Golden Arches logo and McDonaldland characters are globally recognized, popular-culture design classics. Enjoy.

All shirts courtesy of McDonald's golden archives & museums

Opposite above: Ronald McDonald
promotional ringer tee, 1983.

Opposite below: Hamburglar ringer T-shirt, early 1983.
The Hamburglar character was introduced in 1970.

Above: Big Mac promotional ringer tee, 1983. The
Big Mac was first introduced in restaurants in 1968.

Above, top: Ronald McDonald and friends,
circus-style print, early 1980s.

Above: Ronald McDonald T-shirt, 1983. The clown with 'the
smile known around the world' made his TV debut in 1963.

Opposite above: Mac Tonight advertising
campaign tee, 1988.

Opposite below: Mac Tonight advertising
campaign shirt, 1988.

*McDonald's, The Golden Arches Logo, McDonaldland and
the McDonaldland Characters Name and Designs and Mac
Tonight and Mac Tonight Character Design are trademarks of
McDonald's Corporation and its affiliates, used with permission.*

COLLECTOR

PAUL
PAUL'S PLACE, ARCH 53, CAMDEN, LONDON, UK

PM: As a veteran of the vintage clothing trade, what's the best T-shirt you've come across since you've been in the business?

P: A vintage Graceland 1969 memorial T-shirt, Champion label, US football-style… touched by the King.

PM: What's the most popular vintage tee customers request?

P: The most popular was vintage Disney, until every high street shop copied them. New faves include Coca-Cola, Hershey's, DARE, and *the* old fave I Love New York..

PM: Which band shirts are the most common?

P: It must be Def Leppard's Hysteria US tour – Sheffield's finest: five guys, nine arms conquer America.

PM: How do you decide which shirts to keep from the constant shipments you have coming through?

P: I keep certain rock tees that fit: Scorpions (Schenker era), UFO (any), Cheap Trick (pre *Flame*) and any early 1970s Champion football shirts. I'd love a Raspberries or Eric Carmen – any out there?

PM: Your Cheap Trick tees are the most!

Why Cheap Trick?

P: I fell in love with them in 1978 at the time the adverts, clash, 999, and the mighty Chelsea (check out the first LP – tell me I'm wrong!) ruled my world. Then I saw a picture in music mag *Sounds* and my adolescent heart skipped a beat! Who did I love most? The two pretty boys, the accountant drummer? Or the freaky guitar hero? I guess it was Tom Peterson, the bass player, but I still love the harmonies 'n hooks as much today – they never did fit in…. no place, anywhere! A lesson for us all – amen.

COLLECTING & SOURCES

There's no easy way to uncover the kind of gems pictured in this book. Some of the featured shirts are the last-known surviving examples, others are less scarce but you would still have to be prepared to put in the hours to find them. So, whether you want to blow a stash in a vintage boutique store or get your hands dirty at a boot fair or thrift store, you're still going to need lady luck on your side; it's all about the thrill of the chase.

MARKETS & SHOPS

UK:

Camden Stables Market
Chalk Farm Road
Camden Town
London NW1 8AH
Arch 53 is a winner for vintage T-shirts.

Portobello Market
Portobello Road
London W11
www.portobelloroad.co.uk
Friday morning is the best for vintage.

Rellik
8 Goldbourne Road
London W10 5NW
tel: 020 8962 0089
www.relliklondon.co.uk
Vintage boutique selling clothing and accessories from the 1920s to the 1980s.

US:

House of Vintage
3315 SE Hawthorne Blvd
Portland, OR 97214
tel: 503 236 1991

Rose Bowl Flea Market
1001 Rose Bowl Lane
Pasadena, CA 91103
tel: 323 560 7469
Held the second Sunday of every month.

What Goes Around Comes Around
351 West Broadway
New York, NY 10013
tel: 212 343 9303
www.whatgoesaroundnyc.com
Vintage apparel for men, women and children, from the 1860s to 1980s.

ONLINE SHOPPING

Crushi
www.crushi.com
Iron-ons from the 1970s.

Ebay
www.ebay.com
Vintage clothing and accessories.

IronOn Station
www.irononstation.com
Unused, old stock, original transfer-prints and iron-ons from the 1970s and 1980s.

Rusty Zipper
www.rustyzipper.com
Vintage accessories and clothing from the 1930s to 1980s, plus old stock iron-ons.

Wolfgang's Vault
www.wolfgangsvault.com
Music memorabilia, including T-shirts.

DESIGN & RESOURCES

Grateful Dead Art
www.mousestudios.com

Jim Phillips Art
www.jimphillips.com
Rock and skateboard designs.

Powell Peralta & The Legendary Bones Brigade
www.bonesbrigade.com

Thrasher Magazine
www.thrashermagazine.com
Great design resource – view every cover from issue one.

FAN SITES

Kiss
www.kissrocks.net

Nightmare on Elm Street
www.nightmaregloves.com

Public Enemy
www.shutemdown.com

The Runaways
www.runawayssecrets.com

INDEX

Figures in italics indicate the page captions appear

ACKNOWLEDGEMENTS

T-SHIRTS & MATERIALS

We would like to thank the following sources for the loan of T-shirts and archive materials.

Aaron Fisher: 366–7, 469BL, 477, 481B, 488T, 490T

Aaron Lacey: 173, 189, 212–3, 451R, 479BR, 480T

Aco: 128B, 143B, 144–5, 148B, 332T

Anders Eriksen: 434–47

Brian May: 192–9, 414B

Broken Heart Vintage: 472

Calvin Holbrook: 412

Camo Pete: 4, 307T, 316–8, 330, 337B

Cassie Mercantile: 78T, 79, 84B, 148, 250, 451T, 458, 469TR, 474, 479TL, 487B, 488B

Cathy Bryant-Westcott: 410–1

Chris Charlesworth: 127

Colette Robertson: 345

Dean Engmann/shutemdown.com: 394–7

Disney: 475T, MR, BL

Duncan Watkins: 340

François Dirty South: 34T, 35, 54–7, 62–3, 70, 85, 201, 357

Frédéric Gilloutteau: 384

Gary Smith: 297, 309T, 313B

George Castrinos: 150B, 430–1

Helen Stickler/*STOKED: The Rise and Fall of Gator*: 33, 39B, 41–5, 61

Jon Rubin: 158–67

Kelly Smith: 371–2, 376T, 383, 385, 414T

Lynn Berat, Dr: 126R, 132, 134T, 135-9, 150T, 152–3, 184–6

McDonald's: 492–5

Mandy Revill: 341–3

Mark Noble: 39T, 58–9, 102–5, 108, 111–7

Matthew Hawker: 60B

Nick Pankhurst: 177, 484B, 489B

Nik Kukushkin at www.slayersaves.com: 204, 216–7

Ocean Pacific: 76–7, 86–97

Omid: 130T, 181T, 202–3, 205, 214–5, 218, 220, 226–8, 230–3, 235, 239, 242–5, 246, 248–9, 251–67

One of a Kind: 130B, 328, 413, 478, 479TR

Patrick Wheeler: 109–10

Paul Burgess: 294–5, 299, 400–1

Paul's Place, Arch 53, Camden Market: 132BL, 149, 169–72, 174–5, 179, 187, 236–7, 240–1, 319–20, 338–9, 491B

Pete Wilkins: 321–5

Private collector NYC: 126L, 128T, 129, 130B, 131T, 142, 224–5, 276–7, 282T, 283T, 287, 288–9, 300–15, 321–2, 326–7, 333, 368, 476, 482B

Private collector, Arizona: 418–9, 422, 451B, 455, 457, 462–5, 469TL, 470TR, 472

Rob Pugh, Old School Vintage Boutique: 22–3, 34B, 36–7, 60T, 71–3, 219, 221–3

Ron Wilkerson at www.2-hi.com: 118–20

Seditionaries Ltd: 272–5, 278–81, 282B, 283–6, 289–93, 337T, 415

Stephanie Barnett: 189

Steve Gill: 206–9, 229, 247

Stüssy: 64– 8

Sylvia Farago: 412, 483T

Thrasher magazine: 24–31

Tracey Burns: 421B

Vintage Vantage: 15, 401, 404, 407, 432–3

Wayne Standaloft: 370–82

BIBLIOGRAPHY & TEXT CREDITS

Thanks go to the following sources and publications for their extracts and contributions.

430 King's Road text, courtesy of and © Seditionaries Ltd: 272–93

2-Hip introduction, 2-Hip: 118

BMX introduction, courtesy Mark Noble: 98

Kiss captions, courtesy Jon Rubin: 158–67

McDonald's, courtesy McDonald's Golden Archives & Museums: 492–5

Ocean Pacific introduction, courtesy Ocean Pacific: 86

Queen introduction and captions, courtesy Brian May, with thanks to
    Greg Brooks and Richard Gray: 192–9

Ray Stevens, *Fucked Up and Photocopied: Instant Art of the Punk Rock
    Movement*, Bryan Ray Turcotte and Christopher

T. Miller, eds., Ginko Press,1999: 21

Runaways text, courtesy Omid: 254–67

Stüssy text, courtesy Stüssy: 64

Variflex caption, courtesy Matthew Hawker: 60

PICTURE CREDITS

We would like to thank the following sources for their kind permission to reproduce the pictures in this book. All other photographs © Welbeck Publishing, with thanks to Russell Porter.

2-Hip, catalogue ads: 84, 86
Alexandra Giarraputo: 254–7
Anders Eriksen: 434–9
BOMP! magazine: 169, 304, 305
Brian May archive/Richard Gray: 192–9
Chris Charlesworth, rear album sleeve from the *Who's Meaty Beaty Big and Bouncy*: 127T
Corbis Images: Lynn Goldsmith: 454
Determined Productions, Snoopy ads, with thanks to Francis: 449, 450
Disney: 472–5
Frédéric Gilllutteau: 389
Getty Images: Hulton Archive/Dave Hogan: 188
Imagine transfers, Linda Lusardi ad: 17
Jon Rubin: 158–61, 163, 166–7, 234, 238
Kelly Smith: 388
Lisa Carpenter: 158–61, 163, 166–7
McDonald's Golden Archives & Museums: 492–5
Matthew Hawker: 60BL, BR
Omid: 244, 254, 257–8, 260–67
Private Collection: Courtesy of Shout! Factory/Sony BMG Music Entertainment: 269
Private Collector, Girbet, Arizona: 418–19, 422, 451B, 455, 457, 462–465, 469TL, 470TR, 472
Private Collector, NYC: 126L, 128–9, 130, 142, 224–5, 276–7, 282T, 283T, 287, 288, 290, 300–5, 306, 308, 310, 312, 314–5, 321–2, 326–7, 333, 368, 476, 482B
Redferns: 472; Virginia Turbett: 268
Steve Gill: 210–17
STOKED: The Rise and Fall of Gator (2002): /Joel Cherry 21; /Bill Silva Productions 38; /Helen Stickler 30, 33; /Vision Skateboards 40, 44
Stüssy: 64–9
Target Transfers, 1984 youth BMX catalogue ad: 99, 100
Thrasher magazine, covers, T-shirt ads, Thrashirts, Thrashion and *Thrasher* products: 24–5, 28–33
Wayne Standaloft: 386, 390–91

Every effort has been made to acknowledge correctly and contact the source and/or copyright holder of each picture and Welbeck Publishing Limited apologizes for any unintentional errors or omissions, which will be corrected in future editions of the book.

AUTHOR ACKNOWLEDGEMENTS

This book is dedicated to True Love, without which this project would not have come to be.

What started as a romantic notion soon became a daunting journey... we had to call for reinforcements. We were delighted and surprised with the amount of people that not only shared our passion, but were willing to give up valuable time to help us realize this dream. We were bowled over by their generosity, valuable knowledge and, most importantly, their first-class vintage T-shirts.

Firstly we'd like to thank all collector nuts out there – keep the faith – in particular the hoarders who took the time to share their gems with us. Special thanks to Paul from Paul's Place, Mark Noble at Ride BMX, Camo Pete, François Dirty South, Dream Master Anders, Jon Rubin, Steve Gill, and the 'madonnalicious' Kelly Smith, Fred and Wayne.

To Omid the Great: endless thanks for sharing his Monster collection and going the extra mile – keep on rockin'. Also thanks to Rob Pugh, Aaron, Chris Chalesworth, Dean Engman, Nik at slayersaves. com, Pete Wilkins, the anonymous private collector in NYC, Paul Burgess, Siobhan, Zoe, Teresa and Marcus, you're the stars, and Lynn for the shirts and that midnight call that saved us when technology failed.

This book wouldn't have been possible without the help, patience, enthusiasm and expertise of the following contributors. Thanks for taking time out from your busy schedules to photograph and dig up some truly classic, one-of-a-kind designs from your archives: Annouchka and Martin at Target Transfers; Helen Stickler, STOKED: The Rise and Fall of Gator; Ed and Kevin at Thrasher magazine; Alain at Ocean Pacific; Molly at McDonald's; Francis at Snoopy/Determined; Erin at Disney; Matt at Seditionaries Limited; Neil at SonyBMG; Emmy at Stüssy; Ron at 2-Hip.

Additional thanks to Brian May for sharing his rarely seen, rockin' collection of Queen tees and to Greg Brooks and Richard Gray for making it happen.

Where it all began, Notting Hill: thanks to Cassáie Mercantile and One of a Kind for loaning some of their rare treasures.

Thank you to Lisa at Carlton Books for having the faith to commission the book in the first place, for fighting our corner and respecting our wishes to keep it real and not to sell out to the big cheese. Extra-special thanks to Zoë at Carlton for the constant support, both mental and practical – couldn't have got though it without you.

Calvin 'The Sacks' Holbrook, we know it was painful, but we couldn't have done it without you. Alice, the most beautiful girl in the world. And lastly, thanks to Bob and Janet Knee for holding onto the Beano T-shirt for all these years. We'd like to thank all those who helped us down the long and winding road. Apologies to those we may have missed; don't take it personally.